WALKING THE LAKE DISTRICT FELLS

KESWICK

SKIDDAW, BLENCATHRA AND THE NORTH

MARK RICHARDS

CICERONE

© Mark Richards 2020
Second edition 2020
ISBN: 978 1 78631 037 8

Originally published as Lakeland Fellranger, 2012
ISBN: 978 1 85284 546 9

Printed in China on responsibly sourced paper on behalf of
Latitude Press Ltd

A catalogue record for this book is available from the British Library.
All photographs are by the author unless otherwise stated.
All artwork is by the author.

Maps are reproduced with permission from HARVEY Maps,
www.harveymaps.co.uk

Updates to this Guide

While every effort is made by our authors to ensure the accuracy of
guidebooks as they go to print, changes can occur during the lifetime of an
edition. Any updates that we know of for this guide will be on the Cicerone
website (www.cicerone.co.uk/1037/updates), so please check before
planning your trip. We also advise that you check information about such
things as transport, accommodation and shops locally. Even rights of way
can be altered over time. We are always grateful for information about any
discrepancies between a guidebook and the facts on the ground, sent by
email to updates@cicerone.co.uk or by post to Cicerone, Juniper House,
Murley Moss, Oxenholme Road, Kendal, LA9 7RL.

Register your book: To sign up to receive free updates, special offers
and GPX files where available, register your book at www.cicerone.co.uk.

Front cover: Looking down Hall's Fell, Blencathra
Title page: Ullock Pike reflected in Bassenthwaite on a hazy summer day

CONTENTS

Lonscale Fell from Sinen Gill

Key to route maps and topos

 Route on a defined path

Route on an intermittent or undefined path

12 **Starting point**

4 **Route number** (on topos)

▲ **Fell summit** featured in this guide (on maps)

 Fell summit featured in this guide (on maps)

8 **Route number** (on maps)

N

0   500
⊢━━━━┥ m

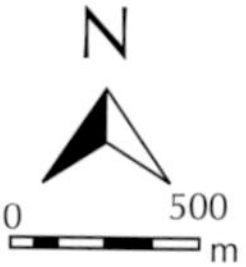

1:40,000

Harvey map legend

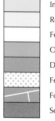

Lake, small tarn, pond

River, footbridge

Wide stream

Narrow stream

Peat hags

Marshy ground

Contours change from brown to grey where the ground is predominantly rocky outcrops, small crags and other bare rock.

 Improved pasture

Rough pasture

Fell or moorland

Open forest or woodland

Dense forest or woodland

Felled or new plantation

Forest ride or firebreak

Settlement

Boundary, maintained
Boundary, remains

On moorland, walls, ruined walls and fences are shown. For farmland, only the outer boundary wall or fence is shown.

Contour (15m interval)

Index contour (75m interval)

Auxiliary contour

Scree, spoil heap

Boulder field

Scattered rock and boulders

Predominantly rocky ground

Major crag, large boulder

O.S. trig pillar, large cairn

Spot height (from air survey)

Dual carriageway

Main road (fenced)

Minor road (unfenced)

Track or forest road

Footpath or old track

Intermittent path

●   ● Long distance path

+ + ⤙ Powerline, pipeline

▪■ ▫ᵘ▫ � Building, ruin or sheepfold, shaft

The representation of a road, track or footpath is no evidence of the existence of a right of way.

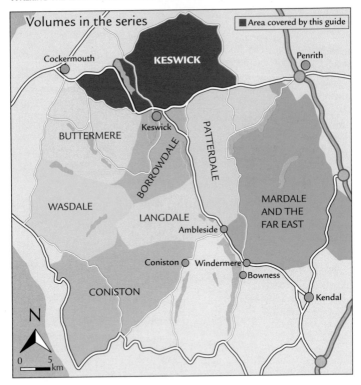

Volumes in the series

Area covered by this guide

KESWICK

Cockermouth

Penrith

Keswick

BUTTERMERE

BORROWDALE

PATTERDALE

WASDALE

LANGDALE

MARDALE
AND THE
FAR EAST

Ambleside

Coniston   Windermere

CONISTON

Bowness

Kendal

N

0   5
km

AUTHOR PREFACE

This land of living dreams we call the Lake District is a cherished blessing to know, love and share. As we go about our daily routines, we may take a fleeting moment to reflect that someone, somewhere, will be tramping up a lonely gill or along an airy ridge, peering from a lofty summit or gazing across a wind-blown tarn and taking lingering solace from its timeless beauty. The trappings of modern life thrust carpet and concrete under our feet, and it is always wonderful to walk the region's sheep trods and rough trails, and to imprint our soles upon the fells. This series sets out to give you the impetus and inspiration to make space in your schedule to explore them time and again, in myriad different ways.

However, the regular paths of long tradition deserve our care. Progressively many of the main paths are being re-set with cobbles and pitching by organisations such as Fix the Fells, to whose work you have contributed by buying this guide. But in many instances, the best consideration we can give these pathways is rest. The modern fellwanderer should show a new 'green' awareness by choosing to tread lightly on the land and to find new ways around the hills. One of the underlying impulses of this guide is to protect these beloved fells by presenting a diversity of route options for each and every fell – and also, in this new edition, recommending 'fell-friendly' routes to each summit which are less susceptible to erosion.

Another feature of this latest incarnation of Fellranger, apart from the smaller size to slip in your pocket or pack, is the addition of a selection of inspiring ridge routes at the end of each volume for those of you who like to spend a little longer with your head and feet in the heavenly realms, relishing the summit views and the connections between the felltops, as well as some accompanying online resources for readers with a digital bent.

Mark Richards
www.markrichardswalking.co.uk

STARTING POINTS

Location			GR [NY...]	Access	Ascents described from here
1	Mousthwaite Comb	Verge parking for 6 cars	349 273	FP	Bannerdale Crags, Blencathra, Souther Fell
2	Scales	Large parking area close to pub and layby	339 267	FP	Blencathra
3	Threlkeld	Village car park up Blease Road	318 256	PP, B	Blencathra
4	Blencathra Centre	Open parking beyond cattle grid	302 256	FP	Blencathra, Lonscale Fell
5	Gale Road	Verge for 20 cars at top of lane, usually crammed	281 253	FP	Latrigg, Lonscale Fell, Skiddaw, Skiddaw Little Man
6	Millbeck	Parking for 5 cars at village hall	256 261	PP	Carl Side, Dodd, Skiddaw, Skiddaw Little Man
7	Whinlatter Pass	Large formal car park	207 244	PP, B	Lord's Seat, Whinlatter
8	Hobcarton	Large forestry parking area	192 245	FP, B	Whinlatter
9	Spout Force	Large forestry parking area	182 255	FP, B	Broom Fell, Graystones, Lord's Seat, Whinlatter
10	Harrot Hill Farm	Tiny verge NW of farm by gill in wood	151 282	FP	Graystones
11	Embleton Church	Verge for 10 cars	163 294	FP	Graystones, Ling Fell
12	Brumston Bridge	Verge for 15 cars between bridge and gate	186 293	FP	Broom Fell, Graystones, Ling Fell, Sale Fell
13	Wythop Church	Verge by church and lower down with scope for 15 cars	189 301	FP	Sale Fell
14	Pheasant Hotel	Generous parking on old road	199 307	FP	Sale Fell
15	Woodend Brow	Compact parking area (donation)	218 276	FP, B	Barf, Lord's Seat, Sale Fell

Location			GR [NY...]	Access	Ascents described from here
16	Powter How	Compact parking area (donation)	221 265	FP, B	Barf, Lord's Seat
17	Old Sawmill Tearoom	Large formal parking area	235 282	PP, B	Carl Side, Dodd, Long Side, Ullock Pike
18	Rabbit Warren	Compact forestry recess with room for 15 cars	234 292	FP	Skiddaw, Ullock Pike
19	High Side	Tiny recessed verge for 5 cars	236 310	FP	Carl Side, Skiddaw, Ullock Pike
20	Peter House	Two laybys for 12 cars (donations to Fix the Fells)	249 323	FP	Bakestall, Great Calva, Skiddaw
21	Skiddaw House	Walk/bike-in youth hostel in the midst of the Northern Fells	287 291	F	Bakestall, Blencathra, Great Calva, Lonscale Fell, Skiddaw, Skiddaw Little Man
22	Horsemoor Hills	Tiny verge for 3 cars	252 334	ask at farm	Great Calva, Great Cockup, Knott, Meal Fell
23	Binsey Lodge	Verge space for 10 cars	235 351	FP	Binsey
24	Keswick Reach	Lots of space on old road parallel to A591 (not at the lodge retreat itself)	207 354	FP, B	Binsey
25	Over Water	Small car park for 10 cars	255 354	FP	Binsey
26	Longlands	Small verge for 6 cars	266 358	FP	Brae Fell, Great Cockup, Great Sca Fell, Knott, Longlands Fell, Meal Fell
27	Greenhead	Lane above farm; room for 10 cars	286 370	FP	Brae Fell, Great Sca Fell, Longlands Fell
28	Fell Side	Open common verge	304 373	FP	Brae Fell, Great Sca Fell, High Pike, Knott

Location		GR [NY...]	Access	Ascents described from here
29	Nether Row	Small grassy triangle	324 377	FP	High Pike
30	Hesket Newmarket	Generous village car park	342 386	FP, B	High Pike
31	Carrock Beck	Verge on common	350 350	FP	Carrock Fell, High Pike
32	Stone Ends	Verge on common	354 336	FP	Carrock Fell
33	Mosedale	Quaker Meeting House car park (donation) and verge	357 322	FP	Bowscale Fell, Carrock Fell
34	Grainsgill Bridge	Verge near road-end	327 327	FP	Bowscale Fell, Carrock Fell, Great Calva, High Pike, Knott
35	Bowscale	Small layby parking area for 10 cars	359 317	FP	Bowscale Fell
36	Mungrisdale	Generous parking area opposite village hall (donation)	364 302	FP, B	Bannerdale Crags, Blencathra, Bowscale Fell, Souther Fell

FP – free parking
PP – pay parking
B – on a bus route (in season)
F – only accessible by foot or bike

A sneaky path bound for Widow Hause breaks off from
a forest track, en route to Broom Fell or Graystones

Bannerdale Crags seen from Bannerdale Head

INTRODUCTION

Valley bases

In the main part, the great mountain massif that looms to the north of Keswick is a lonesome land of rounded common pasture ringing to a symphony of skylarks. No wonder the most northerly fells here, affectionately known collectively as Back o'Skidda, are adored by discerning fellwanderers for their liberty and seclusion. They are merely the backdrop to its two trophy mountains – Skiddaw and Blencathra. Across Bassenthwaite Lake a complementary cluster of smaller fells rises from the conifers of Whinlatter Forest Park, much less visited and offering fine viewpoints for the star attraction, with wide unimpeded views north across the Solway.

Sitting at the confluence of two wide valleys, that of Bassenthwaite Lake to the north and that of the River Greta to the east, Keswick is the ultimate valley base for exploring this rich landscape. The setting is both sublime and handy, giving the sweetest of fell-path approaches to the Skiddaw massif, with the Glenderaterra valley providing access to the quiet roadless country at the headwaters of the Caldew and, further east, onto Scales Fell for Blencathra.

↑ *The Skiddaw massif from a northern ascent of Lord's Seat*

The town also serves as a springboard for short drives or bus journeys via Braithwaite to access the cluster of gentle fells above Whinlatter Forest Park.

The A66 is the main thoroughfare through the Vale of Keswick from Penrith in the east to Cockermouth in the west, while country roads skirt all around the periphery of the Northern Fells to link Bassenthwaite, Ireby, Caldbeck, Hesket Newmarket and Mungrisdale, offering tempting access into the interior from other angles. The Whinlatter Pass, sweeping serenely over from the picturesque Vale of Lorton to Braithwaite, forms the southern boundary of and offers additional access to the Whinlatter Group.

Facilities

As long as you have a car, there are plenty of hotels, self-catering cottages and camp sites scattered across the area, including some established to serve the Cumbria Way which traverses

The Horse and Farrier pub in Threlkeld, underneath Blencathra

the heart of the Northern Fells, although the main concentration is in Keswick and the nearby villages of Threlkeld, Portinscale and Braithwaite. (The Visit Cumbria website (www.visitcumbria.com, click Accommodation) seems to have the best database or you could just use a search engine.) Only in Keswick will you find a petrol station or a supermarket, but there are excellent village shops in Hesket Newmarket, Portinscale, Braithwaite and Lorton.

Getting around

For the carless the X4/X5 bus service is the key to access to Keswick, running between Penrith and Cockermouth via Threlkeld and Keswick, or, from the south, the 555 runs from Lancaster via Kendal, Windermere and Ambleside. For getting around, the twice-daily 73 bus from Carlisle to Keswick via Caldbeck and Bassenthwaite may be of value at the start of a walk, but its timetable is geared more towards shoppers than trekkers. The Honister Rambler 77 bus is nifty for Whinlatter Pass approaches but only runs between spring and autumn.

Parking is not to be taken for granted anywhere in this popular park. The pinch point in this area is along the A66 from Scales round to Bassenthwaite. Always allow time to find an alternative parking place, if not to switch to a different plan for your day or just set out directly from your door – perfectly possible if you find accommodation within any of the main valleys. Always take care to park safely and only in laybys and car parks, not on the side of the narrow country roads. Consult the Starting points table to find out where the best parking places (and bus stops) are to be found. Note that although, in general, one preferred starting point is specified for each route, there may be alternative starting points nearby (for example in the vicinity of Whinlatter Visitor Centre) should you arrive and find your chosen spot taken.

Fix the Fells

The Fellranger series has always highlighted the hugely important work of the Fix the Fells project in repairing the most seriously damaged fell paths. The mighty challenge has been a great learning curve and the more recent work, including complex guttering, is quite superb. It ensures a flat foot-fall where possible, is easy to use in ascent and descent, and excess water escapes efficiently, minimising future damage.

The original National Trust and National Park Authority partnership came into being in 2001 and expanded with the arrival of Natural England, with additional financial support from the Friends of the Lake District and now the Lake District Foundation (www.lakedistrictfoundation.org). But, and it's a big but, the whole endeavour needs to raise £500,000 a year to function. This enormous figure is needed to keep pace with the challenges caused by the joint tyranny of boots and brutal weather. The dedicated and highly skilled team, including volunteers, deserve our sincerest gratitude for making our hill paths secure and sympathetic to their setting. It is a task without end, including pre-emptive repair to stop paths from washing out in the first place.

Bearing in mind that a metre of path costs upwards of £200 there is every good reason to cultivate the involvement of fellwalkers in a cause that must be dear to our hearts… indeed our soles! Please make a beeline for www. fixthefells.co.uk to make a donation, however modest. Your commitment will, to quote John Muir, 'make the mountains glad'.

Bakestall from the Horsemoor Hills track

Using this guide

Unlike other guidebooks which show a single or limited number of routes up the Lakeland fells, the purpose of the Fellranger series has always been to offer the independent fellwalker the full range of approaches and paths available and invite them to combine them to create their own unique experiences. A valuable by-product of this approach has been to spread effects of walkers' footfall more evenly over the path network.

This guide is divided into two parts. 'Fells' describes ascents of each of the 30 fells covered by this volume, arranged in alphabetical order. 'Ridge routes' describes a small selection of popular routes linking these summits.

Fells

In the first part, each fell chapter begins with an information panel outlining the character of the fell and potential starting points (numbered in blue on the guide overview map and the accompanying 1:40,000 HARVEY fell map, and listed – with grid refs – in 'Starting points' in the introduction). The panel also suggests neighbouring fells to tackle at the same time, including any classic ridge routes. The 'fell-friendly route' – one which has been reinforced by the national park or is less vulnerable to erosion – is also identified for those particularly keen to minimise their environmental impact.

After a fuller introduction to the fell, summarising the main approaches and expanding on its unique character and features, come the route descriptions. Paths on the fell are divided into numbered sections. Ascent routes are grouped according to starting point and described as combinations of (the red-numbered) path sections. The opportunities for exploration are endless. For each ascent route, the ascent and distance involved are given, along with a walking time that should be achievable in most conditions by a reasonably fit group of walkers keen to soak up the views rather than just tick off the summit. (Over time, you will be able to gauge your own likely timings against these figures.)

In many instances a topo diagram is provided alongside the main fell map to help with visualisation and route planning. When features shown on the maps or diagrams appear in the route descriptions for the first time (or the most significant time for navigational purposes), they are highlighted in **bold**, to help you trace the routes as easily as possible.

As a good guide should also be a revelation, panoramas are provided for a small number of key summits, and panoramas for every fell in this guide can be downloaded free from www.cicerone.co.uk (see 'Additional online resources' below). These name the principal fells and key features in the direction of view.

Advice is also given at the end of each fell chapter on routes to neighbouring fells and safe lines of descent should the weather close in. In fell-walking, as in any mountain activity, retreat is often the greater part of valour.

Ridge routes

The second part of this guide describes some classic ridge routes in the Keswick area. Beginning with an information panel giving the start and finish points, the summits included and a very brief overview, each ridge route is described step by step, from start to finish, with the summits highlighted in bold in the text to help you orientate yourself with the HARVEY route map provided. Some final suggestions are included for expeditions which you can piece together yourself from the comprehensive route descriptions in 'Fells'.

Appendices

For more information about facilities and services in the Lake District, some useful phone numbers and websites are listed in 'Useful contacts'. 'A fellranger's glossary' offers a glossary to help newcomers decode the language of the fells, as well as explanations of some of the most intriguing place names you might come across in this area. The 'Alphabetical list of fells in the Fellranger series' is a comprehensive list of all the fells included in this 8-volume series, to help you decide which volume you need to buy next!

Safety and access

Always take a map and compass with you – make a habit of regularly looking at your map and take pride in learning how to take bearings from it. In mist this will be a time-saver, and potentially a life-saver. The map can enhance your day by showing additional landscape features and setting your walk in its wider context. That said, beware of the green dashed lines on Ordnance Survey maps. They are public rights of way but no guarantee of an actual route on the ground – as can be observed with the marking of a path striking diagonally up the long steep slope of Blease Fell from above the Blencathra Centre – highly improbable and, in fact, non-existent. Take care to study the maps and diagrams provided carefully and plan your route according to your own capabilities and the prevailing conditions.

Please do not rely solely on your mobile phone or other electronic device for navigation. Local mountain rescue teams report that this is increasingly the main factor in many of the incidents they attend.

Souther Fell from above Mousthwaite Col

An arrow, helpfully created by fellow fellwanderers, shows the way off the track up to Whinlatter south top

The author has taken care to follow time-honoured routes and keep within bounds of access, yet access and rights of way can change and are not guaranteed. Any updates that we know of to the routes in this guide will be made available on the Cicerone website, www.cicerone.co.uk/1037, and we are always grateful for information about discrepancies between a guidebook and the facts on the ground, sent by email to updates@cicerone.co.uk or by post to Cicerone Press, Juniper House, Murley Moss, Oxenholme Road, Kendal, Cumbria, LA9 7RL.

Additional online resources

Summit panoramas for all of the fells in this volume can be downloaded for free from the guide page on the Cicerone website (www.cicerone.co.uk/1037). You will also find a ticklist of the summits in the Walking the Lake District Fells series at www.cicerone.co.uk/fellranger, should you wish to keep a log of your ascents, along with further information about the series.

1 BAKESTALL 673M/2208FT

Climb it from	Peter House **20** or Skiddaw House **21**
Character	Craggy northern end of the Skiddaw massif forming a majestic amphitheatre above Dash Falls
Fell-friendly route	1
Summit grid ref	NY 266 307
Link it with	Skiddaw
Part of	The Skiddaw Skyline

This craggy shoulder is one of the treasures of the Skiddaw massif and fully deserves to be savoured for its own sturdy virtues. It's best appreciated from the north from Dash Beck valley, with the drama of Dead Crags rising above Dead Beck ravine and the spectacular Whitewater Dash waterfall (commonly known as Dash Falls). Under these eastern slopes runs the access track to Skiddaw House – a truly remote mountain hostel, off-grid and off the beaten track.

The great amphitheatre of Dead Crags offers a happy home for raven and peregrine above shy Dead Beck, made more reclusive by recent tight fencing to exclude the sheep and encourage natural regrowth of native trees. Within the ravine lurks scant evidence of a lead mine and some fine cascades in its lower stages, but they are currently inaccessible to the casual fellwanderer.

↑ *Bakestall's northern aspect from the path up Little Calva (photo: Andrew Locking)*

All too many walkers charge up Skiddaw by the fence and miss the aura and magic of Bakestall. Don't be in their number. Allow time for its exclusive pleasures, but wander carefully as the cliffs are real and profound. There are three lines of ascent, with variants, from the north, with only Birkett Edge (4) carrying a regular flow of foot traffic.

Ascent from Peter House 20

Three contrasting routes on grassy highways, one with just a little off-piste action (2) and another offering a stiff direct ascent for the true adventurer (3)

Via Cockup →*3.1km/2 miles* ↑*475m/1560ft* ⏱*1hr 45min*
1 Follow the road southwest, passing **Tenter Hill Farm**. At the right-hand bend short of **Melbecks** leave the road left, following the bridle-lane. After a gate this becomes an open green track. Continue through further gates, rising up the pasture with a wall/fence left to a hand-gate in the intake wall. Follow on up the fellside to come over the shoulder of **Cockup**. A clear path retains the southeasterly line then curves south to ford **Dead Beck**. From here wind easily up the slope to the summit.

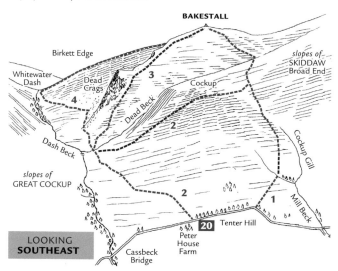

21

Via the Dash valley road →*3.5km/2¼ miles* ↑*455m/1495ft* ◔*1hr 40min*
2 Follow the gated road (southeast) direct from the parking area. Step off the metalled road as a track forks right, following a marker stone, 'Bridleway via Dash Falls, Skiddaw House, Threlkeld'. After the next gate climb the pathless slope (right), mounting onto the western shoulder of **Cockup** and curving round high up to join an increasingly clear sheep path. Follow it on to bend left to join Route **1**.

Via Dead Crags →*2.7km/1¾ miles* ↑*460m/1510ft* ◔*1hr 40min*

A very vigorous, perhaps less-than-intuitive, direct option

3 Set off with Route **2** from Peter House Farm. Instead of turning right at the gate, take the path mounting the obvious groove directly up the fellside. At last the slope eases and the path is lost. Carefully follow sheep trods above the dramatic gulf of **Dead Crags**. Head south, initially carefully following sheep trods, while admiring the view over the dramatic gulf of Dead Crags, peering imperiously down

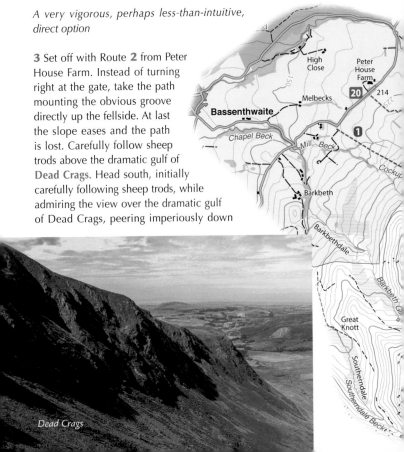

Dead Crags

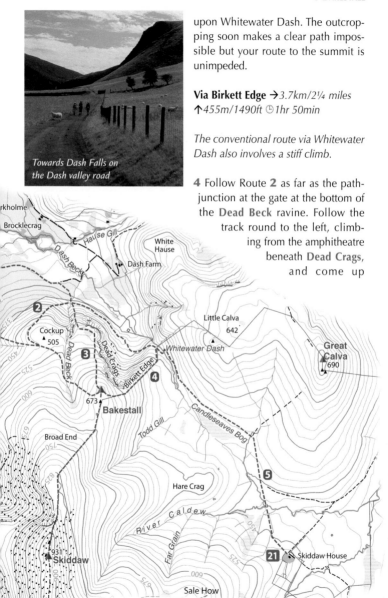

Towards Dash Falls on the Dash valley road

upon Whitewater Dash. The outcropping soon makes a clear path impossible but your route to the summit is unimpeded.

Via Birkett Edge →3.7km/2¼ miles ↑455m/1490ft ⏲1hr 50min

The conventional route via Whitewater Dash also involves a stiff climb.

4 Follow Route **2** as far as the path-junction at the gate at the bottom of the **Dead Beck** ravine. Follow the track round to the left, climbing from the amphitheatre beneath **Dead Crags**, and come up beside the no less impressive dash of white water, which can be a thrilling sight. Just before the next gate leave the supply road to Skiddaw House hostel and step up right, ascending beside the wall, which quickly becomes a fence, and climbing **Birkett Edge**. After a period of diligent climbing watch for a fence-junction to the left. Soon the path splits and a stepped path bends half-right to reach the summit cairn. If you miss this in the mist, follow the main fence-side path which mounts to the cairn at the left-hand fence-corner. Here turn right, following the path down (yes, down) to the summit only 100 metres away.

Ascent from Skiddaw House 21

Via Birkett Edge →*3.8km/2½ miles* ↑*310m/1010ft* ⏱*1hr 30min*

The integral opening move to the Skiddaw skyline

5 Follow the supply track northwest, crossing the footbridge over the **River Caldew** beside the ford and continuing to the gate beside the head of **Whitewater Dash**. Go through and, stepping up left, join forces with Route **4**.

The summit

A substantial cairn forms an attractive foreground to a spacious northerly view far beyond Binsey to Criffel and the distant hills of Dumfries across the Solway. In the opposite direction see Skiddaw peeping to the left of Broad End, as well as Helvellyn and High Street and the northern aspect of Blencathra, with Atkinson Pike the more striking peak. Northwards Dash Farm lies over the lip of Dead Crags, backed by the Uldale Fells and Knott, with Carrock Fell peering over Little Calva.

Safe descents

With the rim of Dead Crags lurking unseen to the NE you need to be alert in mist. The sure course is S to the fence and then down Birkett Edge (**4**) to the Skiddaw House track, turning left for the public road at Peter House or right for Skiddaw House (**5**).

Looking north towards Knott from the summit cairn

Ridge route

Skiddaw →*2km/1¼ miles* ↓*10m/35ft* ↑*270m/890ft* ⏱*1hr 10min*
Step back S to join the fence. The fence-side path soon embarks on a long
steady climb onto Broad End, where the ridge path drifts naturally away
from the fence (as it runs under the east slope of the mountain) to gain the
north top.

2 BANNERDALE CRAGS 683M/2241FT

Climb it from	Mousthwaite Comb **1** or Mungrisdale **36**
Character	Held between the upper Glenderamackin and Bannerdale, an impressive precursor to Blencathra from the east
Fell-friendly route	3
Summit grid ref	NY 335 290
Link it with	Blencathra or Bowscale Fell
Part of	The Blencathra Round

Taking its name from the broken northeast face which casts an afternoon shadow over the head of the valley, Bannerdale Crags is the craggiest of the three distinctly different fells that cluster round the hamlet of Mungrisdale. Hidden away at the top of the vast empty bowl of Bannerdale, it also makes an excellent viewpoint for and precursor to Blencathra, and a focus of the northern approaches beyond Sharp Edge. Connecting Bannerdale Crags and Blencathra and curling round the lesser fell's lower slopes runs the rather grandly named River Glenderamackin – every inch a beck!

↑ *Bannerdale Crags' craggy northeastern aspect*
from Souther Fell (photo: Mike Rowbottom)

At the head of Bannerdale Beck lurk the collapsed entrances to an old lead mine, and high on the east ridge slate was once chipped then hauled by ponies. There are even the foundations of a coyly sited stone bothy, tucked into a tiny alcove round the east side of the ridge.

While Mungrisdale may seem the primary focus and root of ascents (3–5), Mousthwaite Col can play into canny route planning and provide an appealing circuit via White Horse Bent and the Glenderamackin (1–2).

Ascent from Mousthwaite Comb 1

Two routes over Mousthwaite Col make a fine if unexpected circuit, with a good balance of high and low-level exploration.

Via White Horse Bent →*3.2km/2 miles* ↑*485m/1590ft* ⏱*1hr 35min*
1 From the parking area walk up the rise to a footpath sign 'Blackhazel Beck' leading to a kissing-gate. The popular path runs on up **Mousthwaite Comb**, curving and pitching steeply to the grassy saddle of **Mousthwaite Col**. Initially

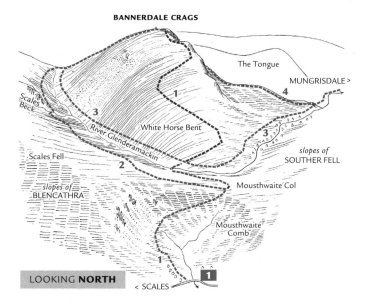

BANNERDALE CRAGS

The Tongue

MUNGRISDALE >

Scales Beck

3

White Horse Bent

River Glenderamackin

Scales Fell

2

4

3

slopes of SOUTHER FELL

Mousthwaite Col

slopes of BLENCATHRA

1

Mousthwaite Comb

1

LOOKING **NORTH**

< SCALES

1

27

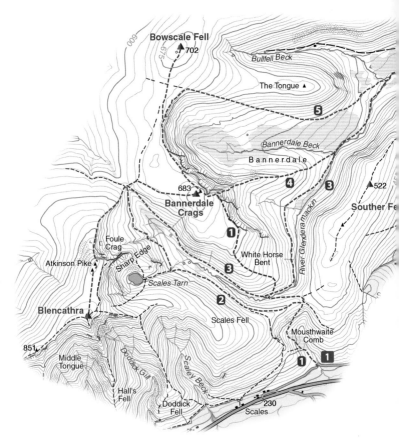

bear right, then after a matter of paces join the sheep trod and cross directly left over the ridge on a path which leads down to a broad wooden bridge spanning the **River Glenderamackin**. Bear up right to meet and spurn the valley path, instead climbing pathlessly straight up the steep grassy slope, passing the prostrate clumps of gorse. Keep slanting half-right to gain the easier slope of **White Horse Bent** and then bear up left to relish a clear view of Sharp Edge and Blencathra. Slant half-right again, traversing to reach the rim of the south-eastern cliff-edge of the fell. Follow the sheep trod to the crest of the east ridge and wander up to the large cairn (the actual summit cairn lies back to the left).

Via the upper Glenderamackin →4.5km/2¾ miles ↑465m/1525ft
① 1hr 45min

2 Follow Route **1** as far as Mousthwaite Col then bear up the gentle gradient of the main ridge on the popular path to Scales Tarn and Sharp Edge. This contours west along the slopes of **Scales Fell**. After fording **Scales Beck** bend back down right on a path which then contours as it passes below Brunt Knott. At a shallow scree indent the main path swings up. The narrow, deeply grooved path can be muddy in its upper reaches as it leads to the saddle at the source of the **River Glenderamackin**. From the headstream saddle bear right on a clear grass path which leads unfailingly to the summit.

Ascent from Mungrisdale 36

Along the Glenderamackin →6.5km/4 miles ↑460m/1510ft ①2hr 20min

Accompany the beck peacefully upstream all the way from Mungrisdale (but expect to get wet feet after really wet weather).

3 Leave the village along the short lane from the phone box. Pass through the gate and embark upon the open track which crosses the **Bullfell Beck**

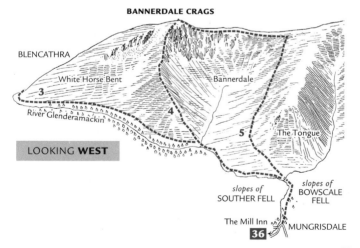

LOOKING **WEST**

footbridge and promptly steps left with the riverside path. The path fords **Bannerdale Beck** with its little waterfall then brushes on through the bracken beside a plantation of deciduous trees. Follow the natural curve of the valley to swing under **White Horse Bent**

Blencathra from the path up the Glenderamackin

and on up the east side of the dale on an agreeable grass path leading to the saddle at the head. Here turn up right to complete the ascent with Route **2**.

Via the east ridge →*3.5km/2¼ miles* ↑*455m/1490ft* ⏱*1hr 45min*

A really splendid climb

4 Start out with the lane from Mungrisdale but just after **Bannerdale Beck** step up the bank and follow the ridge southwest on a clear path. Pass a single

Looking back down the east ridge

wall and the remains of a workshop and, above this, as the crag looms, join a sheep path that contours round the north side of the mountain. Pass another bothy ruin, set on a rock shelf, seldom spotted by walkers heading up the ridge. The regular path keeps to the easy line, avoiding the rock to the left, and soon arrives at the top.

Via Bannerdale →*4.7km/3 miles* ↑*480m/1580ft* ⏱*2hr*

A great turf trail, frequently used in descent

5 Leave the village along the lane from the phone box and follow the open track to cross the **Bullfell Beck** footbridge. Here take the clear bridleway path southwest, taking care not to drift left at a fork on the old track to Bannerdale Lead Mine. Keep to the rising path. Gaining the skyline, swing left along the rim of the great **Bannerdale** amphitheatre, following a marvellous gallery path which leads unfailingly to the large cairn above the main crags.

The summit

Summit cairn

A pitiful cairn marks the actual summit in the grass, and most walkers will ease past it and take refreshment at the large cairn at the top of the escarpment. The view is thoroughly dominated by Blencathra, and while the High Street and Helvellyn ranges also feature, walkers will be intrigued by what they can see over the top of Scales Fell, with Wetherlam, Coniston Old Man, Swirl How and Great Carrs peering round the left side of High Raise, and Crinkle Crags, Bowfell and Esk Pike on the right. There is a long Pennine skyline across the Eden, from Cold Fell to Wild Boar Fell in the south.

Safe descents

All danger lies in the eastern flank of the fell, with no easy lines of descent in mist. For Mungrisdale follow the path NW (**5**) along the rim of the scarp to come upon the descending bridleway which affords an easy line down the northern flank of Bannerdale. The longer option is to head W to Glenderamackin Col, then turn left (SE) with the valley path (**3**), which can also be followed for Mousthwaite Col and Scales.

Ridge routes

Blencathra →*2.3km/1½ miles* ↓*80m/260ft* ↑*260m/855ft* ⊕*1hr*
Walk W, descending to Glenderamackin Col. Ascend SW with the swelling ridge, mounting more steeply S onto Atkinson Pike. Continue S across the saddle, past the pool and quartz crosses, to the summit.

Bowscale Fell →*1.8km/1¼ miles* ↓*50m/165ft* ↑*75m/245ft* ⊕*40min*
Aim NW to reach the large cairn some 80 metres distant from the summit and bend left, faithfully holding to the edge path along the rim of the great escarpment at the head of Bannerdale. Take the first path to trend a little left of the edge, crossing marshy but not deep mosses, to gain the firm footing of the grassy ridge which slopes easily to the summit shelter.

3 BARF 468M/1535FT

Climb it from	Powter How 16 or Woodend Brow 15
Character	Eastern shoulder viewpoint down from Lord's Seat, famed for its white-washed pinnacle, the Bishop
Fell-friendly route	3
Summit grid ref	NY 214 267
Link it with	Lord's Seat

With a presence that belies its small stature, the craggy eastern outlier of Lord's Seat lords it over the southern end of Bassenthwaite Lake. Its steep slopes proudly shaking off the surrounding forestry, its identity is further confirmed by the tell-tale flash of white rock halfway up its flanks.

This white-washed rock on the slopes of Barf is known as the Bishop and originated as a canny piece of publicity by the proprietor of the original Swan Hotel (now the private Swan House) at its foot. In recent years, the role of painting it has been taken over by the Keswick Mountain Rescue Team, who use this landmark pinnacle to remind observers of the important service they perform.

There are three ways up – via the forest edge of Beckstones Gill (1), the 'no holds barred' head-on climb (2) and by the side door of Wythop Woods (3).

↑ *Barf, viewed from the southeast at Thornthwaite, with the little white dot of the Bishop just visible halfway up*

Ascent from Powter How 16

Via Beckstones Gill → *1.6km/1 mile* ↑*370m/1215ft* ⏱*1hr*

1 Walk down the road south from the parking area and take the lane forking right opposite the hamlet of **Powter How**. A footpath sign off this to the right directs through a kissing-gate and along a birch-woodland way, passing the little white-washed rock known as **the Clerk**. The path leads over **Beckstones Gill** to a fence-stile and into the forestry plantation. Join the ascending path, and avoid being drawn too far right into steeper woodland. The actual path is the less obvious one, going more directly up. Come onto cleared fellside

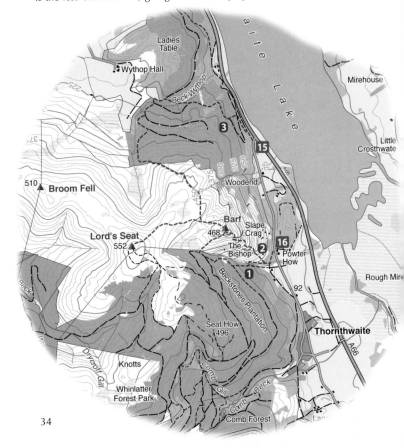

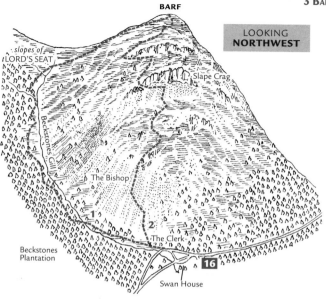

LOOKING **NORTHWEST**

slopes of LORD'S SEAT

Slape Crag

Beckstones Gill

The Bishop

1

2

The Clerk

16

Beckstones Plantation

Swan House

The white-washed Bishop overlooking Swan House

and wind up to meet a forest track. Climb on with this track, watching for the branch right to a fence-stile onto the open fell. Ford the upper feeder-gill and slant right (north-east), stepping onto the shoulder of Barf, where a clear way leads up onto the headland and to the summit.

Via the Bishop → 1.2km/¾ mile ↑365m/1200ft ⏱1hr

The path to the top of the fell is clear if steep, with only Slape Crag to circumnavigate, perhaps with the help of walking poles.

35

2 Begin with Route **1**, branching right onto the obvious scree run at **the Clerk**. Keep labouring up the slope and duly reach the rock pinnacle of **the Bishop**. Continue up the obvious heather-lined path. Watch for the

Oak tree below the narrow shelf left of Slape Crag

walled armchair to the right on a brief level shoulder as you continue climbing through the heather, then bracken. Pass a mature birch and arrive at a patch of scree. Here slant up the bank to come onto the scree spilling from the base of **Slape Crag**.

Slant left and down to find the key rock-step above a spreading oak tree. Fend off the gorse, broom and heather to place your boots carefully on the few awkward rock-steps. The rake is quickly vanquished and the heather trail resumed. It climbs to the base of a ribbed scarp and traverses left to find the easier ground. The upper alps are gained with great elation. Stride through the last heather clumps to the bare rock top and revel in the marvellous view.

Ascent from Woodend Brow 15

Via Beck Wythop →*3.6km/2¼ miles* ↑*410m/1345ft* ⊕*1hr 30min*

A little-used option wending up the forest tracks of Wythop Wood and ultimately onto rough heather moor

3 Follow the NCN 71 cycle route sign to head north with the Beck Wythop road, parallel to the main road. After 50 metres follow a path on the left, signed 'Wythop Hall', initially parallel to the roadway. The path steps up onto a forest track but goes straight over – see the footpath waymark opposite – up through the trees, with one minor rock-step, to reach the same forest track at a higher level. Turn right and follow the track for a further 500 metres, seeking

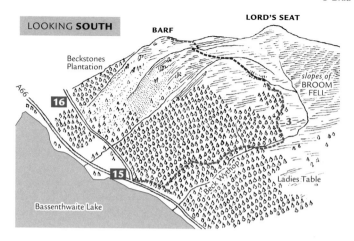

a waymark and a short flight of wooden steps down right. Here the track joins the continuing footpath which leads to a footbridge over **Beck Wythop**.

After this the path rises, still in woodland, to meet a forest track. Turn left and keep with this main thoroughfare track as it meets the track you left at the steps. Sweep right in felled plantation. As the track meets a rougher track on the right, branch up this way, with felled plantation on the right. The track becomes more rutted, angles up into the conifers of Hagg and comes alongside the forest fence. Cross over the tall netting fence at this point onto the open fell and follow the gill left, rising through the shallow ravine to accompany an old broken wall to a wall T-junction. Here bear up right with the wall to find a metal gate on the damp saddle. Barf is in view from here, but is only reached by tramping over the tough moor grass and heather of an intermediate hillock to join the ridge path from Lord's Seat, which leads unfailingly to the top.

The summit

The top is a bare plinth of rock with a grassy surround. Just seven metres to the east is the scarp edge. This is a wonderful perch on which to eat those sandwiches and enjoy a sumptuous view which has no peers, over the Bassenthwaite vale to Skiddaw.

Safe descent

The best way down is via Route **1**, Beckstones Gill. Head SW from the summit on the clear path, stepping down to ford the upper course of Beckstones Gill and cross the stile into the forest. Turn left and follow the track, but watch for the path breaking off down the open felled slope. This winds down, becoming steeper as it enters the conifers. Lower down find a stile on the left which leads back out of the trees and cross the gill again to conclude by passing the white-washed Clerk. Reach the Thornthwaite road opposite Swan House.

Ridge route

Lord's Seat → *1.2km/¾ mile* ↓*45m/150ft* ↑*130m/425ft* ⏱*30min*
A well-etched path leads W and descends to skirt to the right of a damp hollow, before steadily gaining ground as it drifts SW onto the neighbouring felltop, with occasional evidence of old metal fence stakes. Follow on to gain the summit.

Looking back at the Skiddaw massif from the ridge path to Lord's Seat

4 BINSEY 447M/1467FT

Climb it from	Binsey Lodge **23**, Keswick Reach **24** or Over Water **25**
Character	A little volcanic hill set aside from the throng, and a worthy objective for a short family ramble
Fell-friendly route	3
Summit grid ref	NY 225 355

A true individualist, Binsey is a volcanic satellite, set apart from the bulk of the Northern Fells. Access to the uncomfortable terrain of its northern slopes is barred, but it makes a fine objective for walkers of all abilities from other points of the compass. The reward is a grand perspective on the Uldale Fells, the west side of Skiddaw and tiny Over Water, the smallest 'water' in the Lake District and a haven for waterfowl.

Binsey Lodge stands at the southern end of a private drive along the eastern base of the fell, connecting to Ireby Grange in High Ireby. The minor road leading north from the same point leads to the charming hamlet of Ruthwaite (traditionally pronounced 'ruthet') and John Peel Cottage. The huntsman John Peel (made famous by the Victorian music-hall hit 'D'ye ken John Peel') lived here for most of his life on the edge of the Blencathra Fell-pack and Cumberland Hunt fox-hunting territories.

↑ Binsey, viewed from Sale Fell to the south,
across the northern tip of Bassenthwaite

Routes lead up from Binsey Lodge to the east (1), Fell End to the south (2) and the A591 to the west (3), and a delightful 14km low-level circuit takes in an abundance of sites – Over Water, Ruthwaite, High Ireby, the old hunting territory of Whittas Park and even a low rectangular mound that marks the site of Caermote Roman fort.

Ascent from Binsey Lodge 23

Direct → *1.2km/¾ mile* ↑*175m/575ft* ⏱*35min*

Nothing could be sweeter than this route – no more than a stroll.

1 Pass through the hand-gate with the sheep-pens to the right and follow the turf trail irresistibly northwest to the top.

Via Fell End → *1.2km/¾ mile* ↑*215m/705ft* ⏱*45min*

A useful means of creating a circuit (steep in descent)

2 Follow the lane west to **Fell End Farm**. Go through the gate on the right with a bridleway sign close to the farmhouse, adjacent to the stone water trough. The most efficient way is to follow the track right and then bearing left

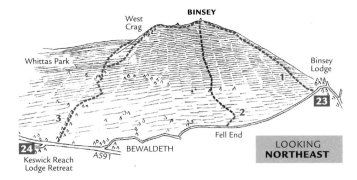

LOOKING **NORTHEAST**

40

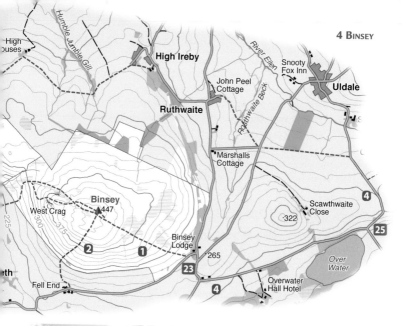

High Ireby

Humble Jumble Gill

High ouses

River Ellen

Snooty Fox Inn

Uldale

John Peel Cottage

Ruthwaite

Roughtwaite Beck

Marshalls Cottage

Binsey ▲447

West Crag

225 300 375

Scawthwaite Close

·322

4

25

2 **1**

Binsey Lodge

265

23

Over Water

eth

Fell End

4

Overwater Hall Hotel

West Crag

of the gorse, then aim pathless up the pasture bank to the hand-gate in the sturdy intake wall at the top. A brief band of bracken and a grass slope with intermittent heather ensue. Head due northeast – there is no path whatsoever yet, for all the steepness, the going is easy enough. As you come onto the ridge-top a path miraculously materialises underfoot, leading by a low outcrop to the summit.

Ascent from Keswick Reach 24

Via West Crag →2.1km/1¼ miles
↑270m/885ft ⏱1hr 10min
3 Walk south along the old road to reach the A591 and cross to take the

gated green bridle-lane leaving it a little to your right. Arriving at the intake wall go through a third gate and follow the path, which skirts to the right of an old pit, passing several ragged thorn bushes. Two lines can be followed, although the more inviting turns to the right of the heather and climbs up under the prow of **West Crag** onto the ridge. The more common path, which follows a braided course, comes up a shallow groove on the north side of the ridge and merges with a green-way coming from **Whittas Park**. Take either, but note that the second option misses the summit. Make sure you visit it, and the northwest cairn, along the way.

Ascent from Over Water 25

Over Water round ramble → *14.2km/9 miles* ↑*475m/1560ft* ⏲*3hr 20min*

A circular tour from the sheltered vale of Over Water

4 From the car park follow the by-road running northeast up Water Bank, signposted 'Uldale and Ireby'. This runs over a brow and gently down to find a bridle-lane on the left. Follow this straight green lane through to the next road. Cross and, a few paces along the facing byway, cross a stile on the right, signed 'Ruthwaite ¼ mile'. Cross the pasture half-left to a stile, and continue into the dell to cross a single-railed footbridge and subsequent stile. Bear half-right via another stile and, following quickly on, a recessed fence-stile, then continue to cross a wall-stile and come alongside a fenced wall. After the next stile, approaching the charming hamlet of **Ruthwaite**, enter the village by a hand-gate between cottages.

Turn up left by **John Peel Cottage**, and at the top go forward with the road above the bus shelter, signed 'High Ireby'. This leads uphill by the lost Ireby Grange into the hamlet. Here take the first left and pass beyond the converted outhouses of the Grange.

John Peel Cottage at Ruthwaite

Curious fireplace and chimney above Whittas Park

At the top bear left into Outgang Lane. This green-way runs down to ford **Humble Jumble Gill**. Subsequently, cross the ladder-stile and advance with the wall close left until after the next ford. As a track, the bridleway goes through a gate and rises, soon coming by the wall, which is now on the right. The track goes down through pasture and reaches a two-way sign-post above **High Houses**. Turn smartly left, keeping with the bridleway as it leads by a small pine copse and goes through a gate, with the wall a constant companion. The track draws away from the wall a little to pass the ruins of a building, probably a hunting bothy, on the craggy brow.

From the Dash valley

Follow the track down to a gate onto the minor road, a short distance below **Caermote Roman fort**. Follow the minor road left to meet the A591 and continue along the broad verge of the main road south, branching off on the old road for sanctuary from the traffic for a while. Where this roadway re-emerges, join the bridleway to follow Route **3** over Binsey, descending east-southeast by Route **1** to Binsey Lodge. At the road junction turn right and keep south down to Whitfield Lodge. Here turn left with the minor road, past the entrance to **Overwater Hall Hotel**. Enjoy the views across **Over Water** as you return to the start.

The summit

A stone-built triangulation column stands beside a sadly mutilated Bronze Age tumulus, thoughtlessly adapted into frivolous shelters. Further west a cairn provides a good outlook towards the coast and Criffel over the Solway. But the actual summit is worthy enough as a place to linger and admire a fabulous view, not only of the Skiddaw massif but also the congregation of fells beyond the Northwestern group to the southeast, into the mountainous heart of the national park.

Safe descents

The principal paths give secure progress in mist, but walkers heading down to the A591 near Keswick Reach (**3**) should be careful not to be lured by the early right-hand fork which leads towards Whittas Park.

5 BLENCATHRA 868M/2848FT

Climb it from	Blencathra Centre **4**, Threlkeld **3**, Scales **2**, Mousthwaite Comb **1**, Mungrisdale **36** or Skiddaw House **21**
Character	Putting on a show above the A66 with great ridges to climb and one notorious razor edge to respect
Fell-friendly route	4
Summit grid ref	NY 323 277
Link it with	Bannerdale Crags or Souther Fell
Part of	The Blencathra Round

Blencathra is a mountain by any measure, among the most revered of all the Cumbrian fells. The iconic two-humped profile seen from points east, which gives it its alternative name of Saddleback, is matched by an imposing southern facade which greets travellers heading through the Threlkeld vale on the A66. Nowhere is that view better enjoyed than on northward journeys through St John's in the Vale. These two perspectives alone make Blencathra an extraordinary fell, quite apart from the riches on offer to those who wish to explore it – be they geologists, historians or mountaineers.

In its entirety, the Blencathra massif is a huge triangle of contrasting fell country most remarkable for its eight ridges, two – Sharp Edge and Hall's Fell – a match for anything in the Cumbrian fells. Of its four summits – (west to east) Blease Fell, Gategill Fell, Hall's Fell and Atkinson Pike – the peak of Hall's Fell is the highest.

↑ *Blencathra's eastern aspect during a winter storm, from the old road west of Troutbeck*

45

It is no surprise that Blencathra has more routes than any other fell in this guide, and none is without merit. From Skiddaw House in the west to Mungrisdale in the east, 11 distinct lines of approach can be identified, with almost as many variants, ranging from gradual grassy approaches (such as Routes 1 and 2) to steep, exposed and rocky scrambles (such as Hall's Fell, 9, and Sharp Edge, 15). Be aware that, although straightforward when climbed in dry settled conditions, in wind, rain or ice the latter become serious mountaineering undertakings.

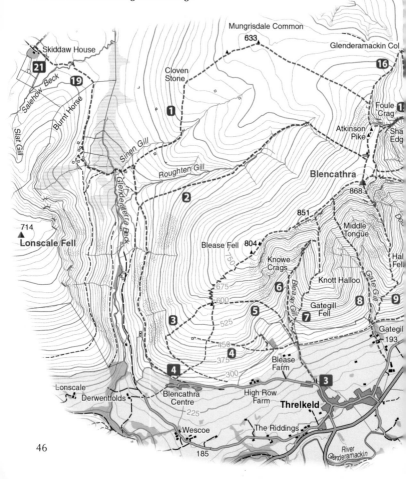

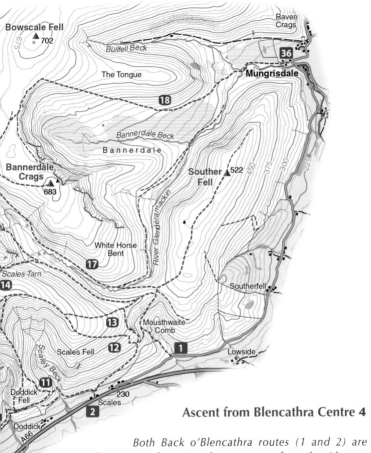

Bowscale Fell
702

Bullfell Beck

The Tongue

36

Mungrisdale

Raven
Crags

18

Bannerdale Beck

B a n n e r d a l e

Souther ▲522
Fell

Bannerdale
Crags ▲
683

River Glenderamackin

White Horse
Bent

17

Scales Tarn

14

Southerfell

13

Mousthwaite
Comb

Scales Fell

12

1

Lowside

Scaley Beck

11

Doddick
Fell

230
Scales

2

Doddick
A66

Threlkeld
Hall

Ascent from Blencathra Centre 4

*Both Back o'Blencathra routes (1 and 2) are
best reserved as quiet descents away from the ridge-top
congregation of walkers.*

Via Mungrisdale Common →6.9km/4¼ miles ↑630m/2065ft
🕓2hr 40min

1 Follow the open track leading on from the car park. This descends
to a restored flag-bridge over **Roughten Gill**. A matter of paces after the

47

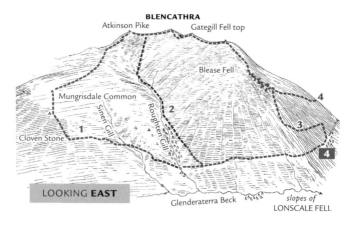

BLENCATHRA
Atkinson Pike   Gategill Fell top
Bleace Fell
Mungrisdale Common
Sinen Gill
Roughten Gill
Cloven Stone
LOOKING EAST
Glenderaterra Beck
slopes of
LONSCALE FELL

concreted flag-bridge notice a stony bank and associated ditch (an old water race). Follow this and, approaching an old fold, bear diagonally up the slope, picking up a quad track. This fords **Sinen Gill** above a marshy patch and before the stony slope intensifies. A clear drove-way snakes up the slope. Follow this but watch to break left and traverse to the **Cloven Stone**, a fine viewpoint. The continuing grassy trail leads on to a cairn and up onto the spongy moor, bound for a solitary cairn, often sitting in a pool of water, marking the top of **Mungrisdale Common**.

Paths radiate from this point. Turn southeast and follow an obvious trail, adorned with cotton grass and pools, over the marshy plateau. Head for the obvious scarp of Atkinson Pike. Join the ridge by a rash of slate, which appears to have been partially quarried and some of it made into a shelter. Now embark on the steady pull up Blue Screes to the cairns on **Atkinson Pike**, and continue due south across the saddle to the summit – passing a pool in the depression and two quartz-boulder crosses laid out on the grass as personal memorials.

Via Roughten Gill →5.2km/3¼ miles ↑620m/2035ft ⏱2hr 40min

2 Set out to round the western flank of the fell with Route **1**, but about 200 metres before the flag-bridge over **Roughten Gill** take a vehicle track swinging up right through the bracken, identified by the large flagstone in the main track. Follow this into the pasture, but watch to keep parallel to the fencing as a faint grass path leads to a hand-gate. Do not go through this but keep close to the fence. Head upstream and walk towards a lonely sheepfold, avoiding the marshy midcourse. At this point turn up the fellside southeast and climb the barren sheep-walk to the saddle of Blencathra, then turn right with Route **1** for the summit.

Via Blease Fell →3.9km/2½ miles ↑600m/1970ft ⏱2hr 15min

A natural elevated launch pad for a traverse that best reveals the magnificence of the fell's escarpment

3 A clear path leads onto the fell from the eastern corner of the car park. Short of a small outcrop come upon a cross-paths. Take the more scenic option which breaks left and, when it ends, follow the popular path bearing up right onto the easy slopes of the fell, rising to a cairn. From this point an engineered trail, with a series of 15 hairpin bends, provides a comfortable means of gaining height up the steep bank of **Blease Fell**. Cairns marshal you to the top and the first jaw-dropping view. The summit lies beyond, along the inviting ridge-way.

Looking northeast along the ridge from Blease Fell

Ascent from Threlkeld 3

You can start any of these routes from the village centre by following the Kilnhow Beck path up to this car park from near the Horse and Farrier pub.

Via Blease Fell →4.5km/2¾ miles ↑700m/2300ft ⏱2hr 45min
4 The gill-side path, signed 'Blease and Blencathra', leads directly up from the car park via a footbridge and steps to reach the open fell at a hand-gate, adjacent to a sheepfold. Here a left turn takes you onto a path which goes through a kissing-gate onto the open fell, climbing an unsightly worn trail. As the slope eases the trail becomes a delightful green trod. Watch for a path crossing and here bear up on a hasty walkers' trail to the cairn to join Route **3**.

    5 An altogether more demanding choice is to start with Route **4** but then continue directly up the fell from the hand-gate. Ford **Blease Gill** and head straight up with a wall on your left. As this swings left skirt the slopes west above the bracken to join the Route **3** zig-zags at the cairn.

Via Blease Gill →2.7km/1¾ miles ↑680m/2230ft ⏱2hr 30min
6 Follow the tree-shaded **Kilnhow Beck** path over a footbridge and up steps, rising to a hand-gate. Head straight up, keeping **Blease Gill** down to the left. Leave the regular path – for Gategill Fell – at a small outcrop before the wall-top, slanting steadily up the grassy slope and admiring the waterfalls of Blease

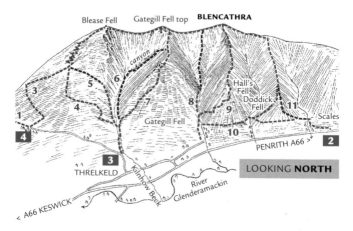

50

Canyon at the head of Blease Gill

Gill and the high rock architecture of Knowe Crags on Blease Fell. At the confluence ford the right-hand tributary and follow the easier heather bank on the north side of the ravine. As this reaches scree move down into the ravine and follow the gill up into the **canyon**. This is a fascinating place, with a rock-band on either side and a ewe-sized cave to the left-hand side. Higher, the gill disappears under a mantel of loose shards and progress inevitably slows. Keep an eye open for a sash of grass draping down on the right. This brings an end to the toil and provides a serene conclusion, climbing onto the Gategill Fell ridge. Complete the ascent with the regular ridge path, either going directly onto **Gategill Fell top** via modest outcropping or following the scree path slanting right to the skyline ridge. Turn right at the top to reach your goal.

Via Gategill Fell →*2.6km/1½ miles* ↑*680m/2230ft* ⏱*2hr 15min*

This is the head-on attack, with the great pyramid of Knott Halloo a strenuous climb through heather, but the ridge beyond is a delight.

7 Follow the gill path up from the car park with Routes **4** to **6**. From the gate head straight on, with the wall to the right. The regular path switches right to reach the top of the enclosure wall and embarks straight up the steep heather bank. When you reach a low lateral retaining wall keep upward (don't let yourself drift right). Climb to the ridge edge overlooking the Blease Gill valley,

51

where the path, something of a slither of scree, becomes more pronounced. Arrival on **Knott Halloo** is a welcome relief. The ridge path is straightforward. The brief narrow spine can be followed or bypassed, and the final rocky crest either taken on or undercut half-right to gain the skyline ridge. **Gategill Fell top** is a grand spot, with more of the character of a mountain summit than Hall's Fell. Follow the ridge right to complete the ascent.

Via Middle Tongue →2.7km/1¾ miles ↑710m/2330ft ⏱2hr 30min

An unfrequented way

8 Reach the centre of the village from the car park by following the **Kilnhow Beck** path down to the pub. Follow the road on through the village, taking a left turn as it bends down to the A66, to follow a quiet lane northeast. Turn up the lane passing **Gategill Farm**, passing through hand-gates to reach the open fell. Follow the old mine path left of the ruin, passing relics of old mine workings. The path, never more than a sheep trod, switches to the east side on the approach to the gill fork, where **Middle Tongue** begins. Ford the right-hand gill and fight your way up through the rank heather and rock on the steep leading nose of the tongue. A sharp headland spells improved going, with the heather less and less a handicap, and the way rises to better grassier slopes. Glance to the left of outcropping higher up to step easily onto the skyline ridge, then turn right to complete the ascent of **Hall's Fell top** (the summit).

Via Hall's Fell →2.5km/1½ miles ↑710m/2330ft ⏱2hr 20min

Keep this ascent up your sleeve for the perfect day. It is the perfect route to the top, a direct climb homing in on the summit. But do not undertake this route if conditions are poor.

Looking down Hall's Fell

The clear path up Doddick Fell

9 Follow Route **8** to the fell gate. From here go forward to ford the weir and step onto the fell's apron. A clear path winds upward – never in doubt, nor too steep. Gaining the crest, the grassy ridge transforms into a rock spine, with scope to grapple or gripe, depending on your mood or the prevailing conditions. Although it is impossible to avoid the airy nature of the ridge in the latter stages, it is possible to make your way around every rock obstacle without using your hands, even if the path is not particularly clear.

Via Doddick Fell →*3.7km/2¼ miles* ↑*730m/2390ft* ⏲*2hr 30min*

A little treasure – especially in September when the heather's out

10 Starting with Routes **8** and **9**, turn right from the fell gate, following the wall-side path through the bracken as it veers upward and leads to the higher ford over **Doddick Gill**. Slant back right to the wall-top. From there the ascent proper begins on a clear path mounting the heather bank to the ridge crest. Turn left and follow the ridge to claim the top of **Doddick Fell**, either direct or by an easier option off to the right. Turn left to reach the ultimate summit.

Ascent from Scales 2

Via Doddick Fell →2.5km/1½ miles ↑640m/2100ft ⏱2hr

A little-known old route across Scaley Beck and onto Doddick Fell, avoiding two uncomfortable rock-steps particularly awkward when wet

11 Take the path up from the parking area to a hand-gate. From here bear left, following the intake wall, approaching the **Scaley Beck** re-entrant. But **be warned**, this crossing is defended by serious rock-steps, the western one the more severe. Instead of tackling these, as you come by a wooden gate in the intake wall find an uncommonly used path rising half-right in the bracken. This path comes over a shelf and contours, with gorse above and below. As the shelf path becomes engulfed in gorse, dip down the short way through the ragged gorse to some slate scree and ford the beck. Clamber up the steep heather bank opposite, crossing the line of an established sheep-track, and continue up the fell onto the ridge-top. Here join Route **10** as it mounts Doddick Fell. (Alternatively, turn left on the sheep-track to contour round to join Route **10** at an earlier point.)

*Looking up to the summit from Scales Fell in winter
(photo: Andrew Locking)*

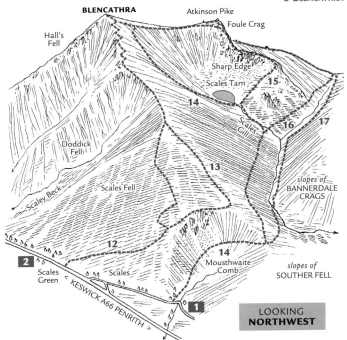

BLENCATHRA

LOOKING
NORTHWEST

Via Scales Fell →3.5km/2¼ miles ↑640m/2100ft ⊕2hr 10min

12 From the hand-gate above **Scales Green** bear right with the popular path slanting up the fellside. As this comes above **Mousthwaite Comb** it switches left and, passing a spring, is released from the bracken to aim for the high ridge, the busy summit never in doubt. **13** Alternatively, continue around the ridge above Mousthwaite Col and follow the natural ridge due west to reach the top of **Scales Fell** by curving round the skyline edge. Where the path steepens it has been re-engineered to reduce wear and tear. Turn right with Route **12** to the summit.

Ascent from Mousthwaite Comb 1

Via Scales Tarn →3.7km/2¼ miles ↑625m/2050ft ⊕2hr 15min

14 Step back west from the car park to find a kissing-gate, from where a path leads, slanting gently up the steep dalehead to the grassy saddle. Turn left with the path to contour above the grooved slope, continuing up the **Glenderamackin** valley to ford **Scales Gill** and reach the outflow of **Scales Tarn**. Another path leads on steadily and stoically southwest to the plateau edge, avoiding the regular Scales route. Turn left at the top to gain the summit.

Via Sharp Edge →4.2km/2½ miles ↑625m/2050ft ⏱2hr 45min

This exhilarating route, one of the very best in the Lake District fells, demands level-headedness and a competence on exposed rock. It is a graded scramble, and the crux – just where the razor ridge meets the slabby wall of Foule Crag – must be respected. Please do not attempt this approach in windy, wet and/ or icy conditions. A fall from the ridge could be fatal.

15 Follow Route **14** as far as **Scales Tarn**. Here your path veers right and eases up to where the **Sharp Edge** outcrops begin. The most exciting route keeps as close to the spine as possible, although many walkers use a lateral path on the

The exposed section of Sharp Edge looking down on Scales Tarn

A walker tackling Foule Crag

northern flank. Both routes eventually take to the slabs to reach the razor edge. A notch or two and a smooth ridge-top slab herald the awkward imposing block at the western limit. Pass this on the north side, with the small slick slab underfoot, to reach the final notch, and step down then up onto the start of the steep slabs of **Foule Crag**.

It's all steady hand-work from this point on, with all manner of options to entertain, until you reach the fell pasture. The main path runs along the brink to the summit, but there is also the worthy option of completing the ascent to **Atkinson Pike** – the natural apex of a remarkable line of ascent – before continuing south to the summit proper.

Via Atkinson Pike →5.2km/3¼ miles ↑660m/2165ft ⏱3hr

16 Follow the **Glenderamackin** valley with Route **14** until you reach **Scales Gill**. Ford it carefully and bend down on a path contouring under Brunt Knott. The path is deeply grooved and can be muddy higher up but leads assuredly to the saddle at the source of the beck. Turn sharp left up the swelling ridge. A rash of slate with a shelter marks a point where you can step left on a small spur to admire the profile of Foule Crag and Sharp Edge. Now embark on the steady pull up Blue Screes to the cairns on **Atkinson Pike** and continue due south across the saddle to the summit with Route **1** – passing a pool in the depression and two quartz-boulder crosses laid out on the grass as private memorials.

Via the upper Glenderamackin →*5km/3 miles* ↑*665m/2180ft* ⏱*3hr*

The better of the two options from Mousthwaite Col

17 Reaching Mousthwaite Col with Route **14**, dip down to cross the plank footbridge and join the grass path leading up the east side of the valley. This continues unhindered to reach **Glenderamackin Col** and join Route **16** to the summit.

Ascent from Mungrisdale 36

Via the Tongue →*6km/3¾ miles* ↑*715m/2345ft* ⏱*3hr 15min*

A good option for the outward line of a round trip, returning initially via Sharp Edge, Scales Tarn, Scales Fell, the Glenderamackin valley or even over Souther Fell

18 The primary ascent from Mungrisdale is the bridleway that slants up the southern flank of the **Tongue**. Take care not to fork left halfway up its slopes onto the dead-end track to the old mine. Once at the top, simply trace the rim of **Bannerdale**, bearing off southwest to join the ridge path from Bowscale Fell and then follow it down to **Glenderamackin Col** and on to the summit with Route **16**.

Ascent from Skiddaw House 21

Via Mungrisdale Common →*7km/4½ miles* ↑*520m/1705ft* ⏱*2hr 50min*
19 From the hostel take the bridleway departing east through the Glenderaterra valley for Threlkeld and Gale Road, crossing the Salehow Beck footbridge and going through a gate at the foot of the Burnt Horse ridge. Turn south on the popular bikers' trail to come alongside a wall. At the obvious fork after a fold bear left and descend to a hand-gate and plank-bridge over the juvenile **Glenderaterra**. Cross the next watercourse, **Sinen Gill**, leave the track and ascend northeast to unite with Route **1** above a ruin and a fold and quickly pick up a clear drove-way.

The summit

Scarp top of Gategill Fell

The benchmark ring, installed by the Ordnance Survey, is all that marks this spot. The view is everything you would expect – airy, extensive and utterly absorbing. The greatest concentration of interest is inevitably held within the southern arc, framed by the mighty escarpment, with the Northwestern Fells clustered above the intermediate Gategill Fell top.

Safe descents

It is possible to wander off the top anywhere in the northwestern arc and come down into the Roughten Gill valley (**2**), with only steep grassy slopes to contend with. But the best options lie at either end of the main escarpment, with Scales Fell (E, **12**) and Blease Fell (SW, **3**) the surest lines. Avoid the obvious ridge beneath your feet (Hall's Fell) if the weather is windy or wet.

Ridge routes

Bannerdale Crags →*2.3km/1½ miles* ↓*260m/855ft* ↑*80m/260ft* ⊕*1hr 15min*
Walk due N, passing through the saddle depression to reach Atkinson Pike. A clear path dips off the northwest lip down Blue Screes, keeping to the edge, which angles NE to the depression at the head of the Glenderamackin. On the rise take the right-hand fork path which leads E to the summit.

Souther Fell →*4.2km/2½ miles* ↓*440m/1445ft* ↑*100m/330ft* ⊕*1hr 40min*
Head E from the summit on the popular engineered path leading down to Scales Fell. As the skyline edge curves SE trend off on the regular path down to Mousthwaite Col. Cross the grassy saddle on a clear path which rises and moves NE, reaching the summit 1.6km (1 mile) from the saddle.

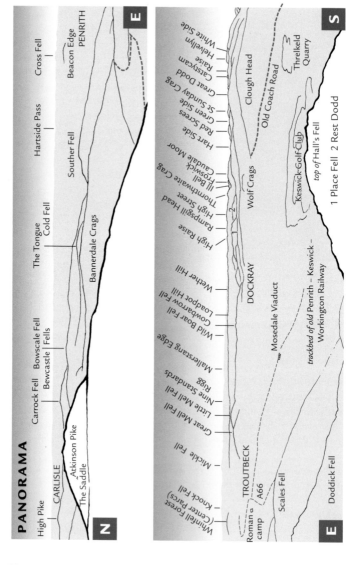

PANORAMA

N

High Pike · CARLISLE · The Saddle · Atkinson Pike · Bewcastle Fells · Carrock Fell · Bowscale Fell · Bannerdale Crags · Cold Fell · The Tongue · Souther Fell · Hartside Pass · Beacon Edge · PENRITH · Cross Fell

E

Whinfell Forest (Center Parcs) – Knock Fell · Roman camp · A66 · TROUTBECK · Micklе Fell · Great Mell Fell · Little Mell Fell · Nine Standards · Rigg · Mallerstang Edge · Wild Boar Fell · Cowbarrow Hill · Loadpot Hill · Wether Hill · Mosedale Viaduct · High Raise · Rampsgill Head · High Street · Thornthwaite Crag · Ill Bell · Froswick · Caudale Moor · Hart Side · Red Screes · Green Side · St Sunday Crag · Great Dodd · Catstycam · Raise · Helvellyn · White Side · DOCKRAY · Wolf Crags · Clough Head · Old Coach Road · Threlkeld Quarry · Keswick Golf Club · trackbed of old Penrith – Keswick – Workington Railway · Doddick Fell · Scales Fell

S

top of Hall's Fell

1 Place Fell 2 Rest Dodd

E

PANORAMA

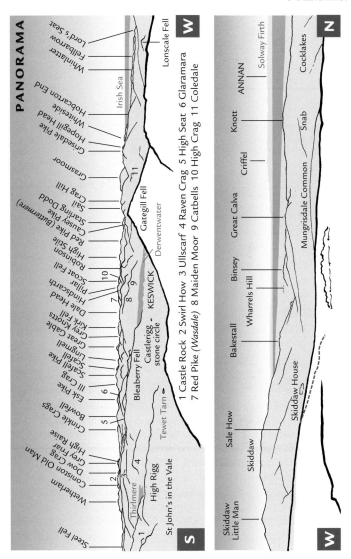

W

Lord's Seat
Whinlatter
Fellbarrow
Hobcarron End
Whiteside
Hopegill Head
Grisedale Pike
Grasmoor
Irish Sea
Lonscale Fell

1 Castle Rock 2 Swirl How 3 Ullscarf 4 Raven Crag 5 High Seat 6 Glaramara
7 Red Pike (Wasdale) 8 Maiden Moor 9 Catbells 10 High Crag 11 Coledale

Crag Hill
Sail
Starling Dodd
Causey Pike
Red Pike (Buttermere)
High Stile
Robinson
Scoat Fell
Pillar
Hindscarth
Dale Head
Great Gable
Grey Knotts
Kirk Fell
Lingmell
Scafell
Scafell Pike
Esk Pike
Ill Crag
Bowfell
Cinkle Crags
High Raise
Grey Friar
Dow Crag
Conison Old Man
Wetherlam
Steel Fell

Gategill Fell
Derwentwater
KESWICK
Bleaberry Fell
Castlerigg - stone circle
Tewet Tarn
High Rigg
St John's in the Vale
Thirlmere

S

N

Solway Firth
ANNAN
Knott
Criffel
Great Calva
Binsey
Bakestall
Sale How
Skiddaw
Skiddaw Little Man
Cocklakes
Snab
Mungrisdale Common
Wharrels Hill
Skiddaw House

W

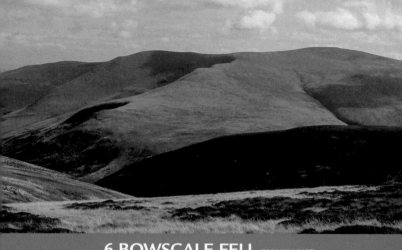

6 BOWSCALE FELL 702M/2303FT

Climb it from	Grainsgill Bridge **34**, Mosedale **33**, Bowscale **35** or Mungrisdale **36**
Character	Rounded fell of heather and fell pasture with a crater-like corrie tarn
Fell-friendly route	9
Summit grid ref	NY 333 305
Link it with	Bannerdale Crags
Part of	The Blencathra Round

The grassy northern slopes of shapely Bowscale Fell (traditionally pronounced 'Bowscil') form the northernmost part of the Blencathra massif. This epic triangle of fell country runs out at the River Caldew as the river breaks out of the mountains to head north to Carlisle. At the same time, to the south of the fell, the Glenderamackin makes good its escape, in this case turning south to reach the Irish Sea via the Vale of Keswick and the Derwent.

Tucked up on the fell's northern flank, in a glacial hanging valley, is Bowscale Tarn, a serene place to idle on summer's days and a popular tourist destination in Victorian times. Directly east of the summit, the V-shaped valley of Bullfell Beck separates the parent fell from the Tongue, a shapely eastward spur. For a moment in the 1980s there were plans for another memorable feature – a dale-bottom safari park west of Mosedale – which fortunately floundered!

↑ *Bowscale Fell, seen from the Cumbria Way, south of High Pike*

While the north and west slopes are largely plain grass, with a patch of juniper west of the Roundhouse facing Carrock Fell, the southern flanks are delightfully clothed in heather. Routes rise up from all points of the compass – along the Caldew from the north and west (1–3), up grassy slopes from the east (4–8) and via Bannerdale to the south (9–10).

Ascent from Grainsgill Bridge 34

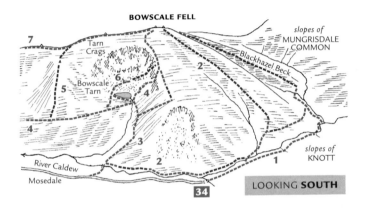

Via Blackhazel Beck →4.8km/3 miles ↑415m/1360ft ⏱2hr

A quiet fell-country wander – best done when the Caldew is low

Blackhazel Beck

1 Follow the bridle-track upstream beside the **River Caldew**. There are two fording places: the first, beyond a barrier, on a vehicular route up to a sheepfold, and the second, more natural for walkers, at the point where **Burdell Gill** enters the river. A path

63

leads on upstream beside **Blackhazel Beck**, passing a roofless ruined bothy. The path can be wet, and after another ford it is lost at the large sheepfold set up on a moraine. Climb the western slope, picking up the trace of a path only after the final hint of a gully is gone. The route levels onto the ridge to come across the ridge path. Here turn left to the summit.

Ascent from Mosedale 33

Via the Caldew and broad west ridge →*8km/5 miles* ↑*475m/1560ft* ⏱*2hr 30min*

A way less travelled ventures upstream, continuing the valley trek.

2 Take the road west from the hamlet for about a mile to reach the **Roundhouse** (a modern house hidden in rhododendrons). Follow the access track down over a cattle grid and by the traditional farmstead to cross the Caldew footbridge. The early track is prone to waterlogging. Once beyond the shelter-belt find sheep trods in the bracken that keep between the river and a mire. The path becomes more evident again as the tumultuous river leaps through rocky constrictions. After the confluence with Grainsgill Beck the path is less certain until the shepherds' track is met at a ford. Follow the track up, fording **Long Gill**, to reach a large sheepfold and continue up the fellside southeast direct to the summit!

Direct →*6km/3¾ miles* ↑*455m/1500ft* ⏱*2hr 15min*
3 Start out with Route **2** but from the **Roundhouse** follow the clear path straight up the fell. As you climb you will (unknowingly) pass a rotunda hidden by rhododendrons visible only from higher up the facing Carrock Fell. Most walkers complete the climb via Bowscale Tarn, but the easier way by far is to head back right at a prominent sheep-trod cross-ways and

slant onto the ridge on a shepherds' drove. Plod up the ridge, short of any outcropping, on comfortable turf all the way to the summit.

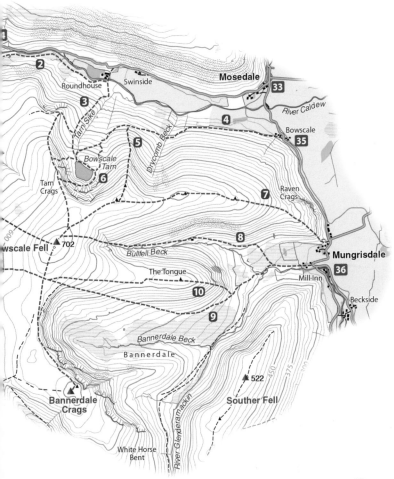

Ascent from Bowscale 35

Via the Bowscale Tarn track → *3.9km/2½ miles* ↑*470m/1540ft* ⏱ *1hr 45min*

Follow the old tourist pony track to picturesque Bowscale Tarn and beyond.

4 Set off from the parking area and leave the road where it sneaks through between the houses. Head along the track west and rise easily across the slopes. When you reach the tarn, ford the outflow and make your way up the rather rotten path west onto the **Tarn Crags** skyline. Here turn left up the ridge to the summit. **5** Alternatively, after fording **Drycomb Beck** and before the tarn, turn south to tackle the east ridge directly without a path. Reach a subsidiary peak and turn southwest to the summit. **6** Or, closer to the outflow, break from the approach track up a path to skirt the eastern edge of the tarn. A path rises easily up the tiered back wall of the tarn, and, although it fades on earthy scree, there is no difficulty in reaching the corrie rim. Turn left with Route **3** to the summit.

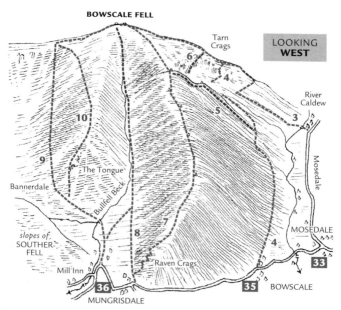

Looking down on Bowscale Tarn

Ascent from Mungrisdale 36

Via the northeast ridge →*3.4km/2 miles* ↑*480m/1575ft* ⏱*1hr 45min*

The east ridge is the conventional and natural first choice, pairing well with Route 8 for a circuit combining ridge and valley.

7 Follow the road on (about half a kilometre) through Mungrisdale to the junction north of St Mungo's Church. Go through the gate behind the houses and pass an old quarry to rise through the gorse on a steep winding course. Each rise in the ridge is crowned by a cairn, drawing walkers irresistibly to the summit with consummate ease.

Via Bullfell Beck →*3.1km/2 miles* ↑*460m/1510ft* ⏱*1hr 30min*

A pathless choice for the solitary lover of lonely fellsides

8 Follow the short lane between charming cottages to pass through a gate and enter the valley. An open track leads on. Take the path that traverses the rushy pasture to the northwest, leaving the valley track at the point it comes close to the **Glenderamackin**. This duly reaches the direct fell-foot track, which heads up into the valley, passing to the right of the waterworks building and advancing above a sheepfold, from where only sheep trods prevail to the dalehead. Scramble across the beck as it cascades over lovely falls, before tackling the steep final headwall, using the heather for handholds, then head straight up west to the summit.

Via Bannerdale → *3.8km/2½ miles* ↑*470m/1540ft* ⏱*1hr 40min*

The most comfortable ascent of all

9 Take the valley track with Route **8**. Cross the simple plank footbridge and keep to the obvious track climbing to the left of the **Tongue**. A minor lateral fork left, halfway up, leads to the forgotten relics of Bannerdale Lead Mine and a

Edge path heading off to Bannerdale Crags

dead end. Keep to the rising line to gain the ridge, where the marshy plateau gives way to dry turf. Aim right, straight for the summit.

Via the Tongue → *3.7km/2¼ miles* ↑*490m/1610ft* ⏱*1hr 40min*

Tackle the Tongue almost head on.

10 Set off with Route **8** to take the valley track, cross the footbridge and carry on towards the nose of the Tongue. Look out for a faint path, hard to spot in bracken season, that breaks up right from the bridleway to climb close to the outcropping very steeply onto the crest, where there is a neat cairn. From here keep to the southern edge of the heathery ridge-top. A sheep trod leads confidently on, linking to a very evident grassy groove which joins the bridleway as it closes in on the ridge-top. Turn right with Route **9** to the summit.

The summit

The precise top is crowned with a low shelter, barely sufficient to give more than bleak respite from a chilly breeze. There is a cairn some 150 metres to the north. The open situation gives extensive views to the fells of the Caldew basin, the Back o'Skidda interior. The Atkinson Pike aspect of Blencathra dominates, while Bannerdale Crags projects its strong craggy face across the long corrie rim of Bannerdale.

Safe descents

West from the summit lie plain grass slopes of a regular angle, but unless the river is low you will need to track downstream to the Roundhouse footbridge (**2**) to gain the comfort of a road. Heading NE from the summit (**7**) stick to the spine of the ridge (E) for a steady descent to Mungrisdale. Alternatively, head S, then as the ridge flattens head E with the bridle-path (**9**) down the flanks of Bannerdale to the same destination. But beware the craggy rim of Bannerdale should you venture too far south, and to the north be wary of Tarn Crags.

Ridge route

Bannerdale Crags → *1.8km/1¼ miles* ↓*75m/245ft* ↑*50m/165ft* ⏲*35min*
Walk S and the dry turf trail comes onto a marshy plateau. Taking the faint left bias, fork to join the path rounding the rim at the head of Bannerdale. An impressive promenade, this leads to the large cairn at the top of the crags, while the actual summit, a more modest collection of slatey stones, lies back some 80 metres SW.

7 BRAE FELL 586M/1923FT

Climb it from	Longlands **26**, Greenhead **27** or Fell Side **28**
Character	The final flourish of the pastoral ridge running down from Great Sca Fell
Fell-friendly route	2
Summit grid ref	NY 288 351
Link it with	Great Sca Fell

Made up solely of barren grass slopes, the greatest merit that Brae Fell can lay claim to is as a viewpoint commonly reached towards the end of a round of the Uldale Fells. The six little summits together form the northwestern corner of the Northern Fells, facing towards Silloth and the mouth of the Solway Firth and making up for their lack of drama with a magical sense of isolation even on sunny weekends.

To introduce a little diversity to the fell, the Wealth of Wildlife Scheme is establishing native woodland on its lower flank, on the east side of Dale Beck beneath Hay Knott. Sadly the fell's only point of geographical interest, the curious ridge of Saddleback in Charleton Gill, cannot be accessed. Easy routes on clear paths converge on the summit from each of the three hamlets to the north.

↑ *Brae Fell from Baggra Yeat, just north of Longlands*

Ascent from Longlands 26

Follow the gill all the way on clear paths.

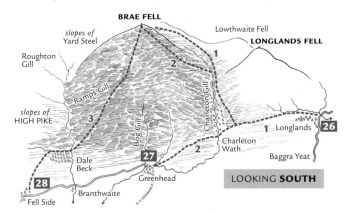

Via Charleton Gill →4.4km/2¾ miles ↑380m/1245ft ☉1hr 30min
1 From the access gate at the foot of the hill in the hamlet of Longlands follow the open track. The green-way rises to come over the brow at the tip of Longlands Fell's north ridge. Here look for a low wooden sign directing half-right, off the track. A regular path, used by quad bikes, rises up the **Charleton Gill** valley, keeping above the ravine. This old way comes above the gill-head, avoiding Broad Moss, onto the wide pasture ridge. Swing gently southeast but watch keenly for the point where the thinner ridge path off Lowthwaite Fell strikes across. Go left with this path, rising east then curving north to the summit cairn.

Ascent from Greenhead 27

Via Charleton Gill →3.6km/2¼ miles ↑355m/1165ft ☉1hr 25min
2 From the parking area by the delightfully named Burblethwaite Beck in the hamlet of Greenhead, follow the open road leading southwest and passing Howburn. At the fork the road becomes a track, signed 'Public Way, Longlands and Cumbria Way'. Follow this to cross the **Charleton Gill** ford.

Charleton Gill ford

Advance to where a low wooden sign directs acutely left onto the fell pasture and follow this to join Route **1**. After about a kilometre, where the track kinks slightly to the left directly east of the summit of Longlands Fell, follow an informal path contouring awkwardly into Charleton Gill. Ford the gill and head up a flat ridge onto the steep west flank of the fell to climb direct to the summit cairn.

Ascent from Fell Side 28

Make a beeline for the summit up the northeastern slopes.

High Pike from the summit

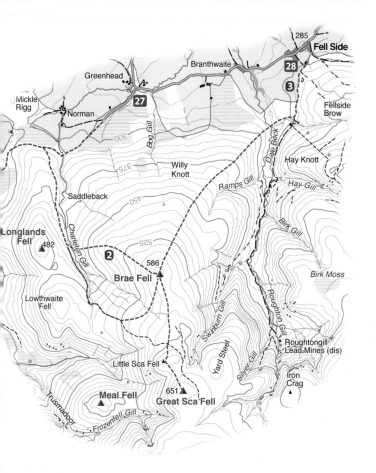

Over Dale Beck →*3km/2 miles* ↑*345m/1130ft* ⏱*1hr 20min*

3 From the parking space go through the fell gate and follow the old mine access track right. Continue beyond the wall-end, with a fenced area of woodland planting right. Where this fence ends bear right, descending on a path that is periodically grooved by trail bikers and coming down to a broad ford of **Dale Beck**. Setting foot on the base of Brae Fell a strong path leads on up the slope. Keep to the right-hand path at a fork and climb easily up the grassy slope to the summit cairn.

The summit

The summit has a definite ridge-end situation, marked by a substantial cairn with a small shelter just below. The summit shares with Longlands Fell and High Pike the majestic northward view towards Carlisle, the Solway and the hills of Dumfries and Galloway.

Safe descents

In mist wet feet will be your only cause of dismay should you stray down the northern slopes in search of the Greenhead to Longlands track.

Ridge route

Great Sca Fell →*1.6km/1 mile* ↓*15m/50ft* ↑*85m/280ft* ⏱*30min*
A simple grass path leads S for 1km to meet up with a bridle-path rising from the Charleton Gill valley, then climbs the steeper slope ahead to reach the brink cairn on Little Sca Fell. The palpable ridge path continues SE, through a shallow depression, en route to the higher top.

Brae Fell summit cairn

8 BROOM FELL 511M/1676FT

Climb it from	Spout Force **9** or Brumston Bridge **12**
Character	A grassy crest on the lovely ridge between Lord's Seat and Graystones
Fell-friendly route	1
Summit grid ref	NY 194 272
Link it with	Lord's Seat or Graystones
Part of	The Aiken Beck Horseshoe

Were it not for the handsome summit cairn, the rambler might be forgiven for reckoning this grassy height little more than the northwestern arm of the Lord's Seat ridge connecting through Widow Hause with Graystones. Yet it is a grand halting place. To either side of the fell are two contrasting valleys, the quiet worlds of Aiken Beck, where conifers are gradually being felled, and Wythop Beck, with pasture farms backed by lovely woodlands and the expansive damp hollow of Wythop Moss at the fell's foot.

Keen eyes will spot at Old Scale the remarkable and, for this locality, unusual pattern of cultivation terracing on the great bank directly behind the farm buildings. What agricultural and social history does this betray?

↑ *Broom Fell from the top of the Aiken Beck valley*

Two routes (1–2) make their way up through the forestry from Whinlatter Pass. A longer approach from the north is also available (3) for those who don't mind getting their boots wet.

Ascent from Spout Force 9

Via Spout Force and Widow Hause → 3.6km/2¼ miles ↑440m/1445ft ⏱ 1hr 30min

A route of two aspects – forested dell and lark-inhabited fell

1 Follow the footpath signed direct from the car park via a stile, coming by the edge of the field to a hand-gate and so down a steep zig-zag flight of steps to cross two footbridges to meet up with and turn right along the path beside **Aiken Beck**. (You could also reach this point from the parking area in the bend of the road at **Scawgill Bridge**.) Embark on the flight of steps and watch for the spur leading to a fenced observatory, the only safe view you can get of Spout Force and its rocky ravine. Otherwise, keep left with the protective fencing above the ravine and pass on and down to the beckside. The winding path moves upstream but not close to the beck, weaving through fallen

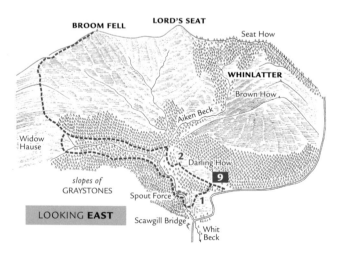

trees and undergrowth to emerge at last onto a forest track in mature conifers. Turn right and keep left at the first track fork, taking the main track up the re-entrant valley. At the second junction follow on round the curve of the track to encounter a felled area, skip over the gill and weave up the inner edge of the stand of mature trees to reach the ridge-top in the eastern depression of **Widow Hause**. Clamber over the fence/broken wall. Join the ridge path ascending east onto the fell, where a level section leads to a final brief climb to the summit cairn.

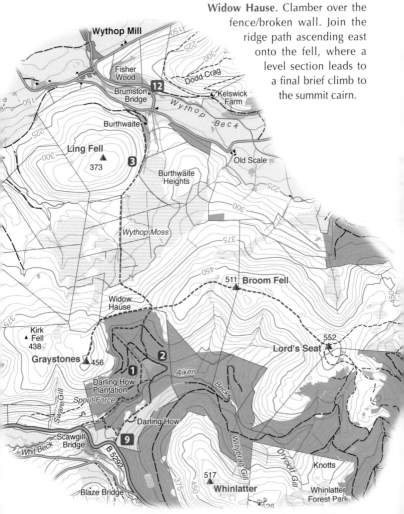

Via Darling How and Aiken Beck →*3.2km/2 miles* ↑*310m/1015ft*
⏱ *1hr 20min*

The quickest way to the top

2 Follow the open forestry track, passing the barrier close to **Darling How** farm. As the track gently descends watch to bear left with the forest track (junction post 28) which then bears right to cross **Aiken Beck** bridge. Shortly the track switches left. At the next fork (junction post 29) look right to spot a humble footpath climbing the bank. Follow this path, which rises easily through the young conifers to meet up with Route **1** on the lateral forest track, and follow the open ridge naturally up right to the summit.

Ascent from Brumston Bridge 12

Via Wythop Moss →*6.4km/4 miles* ↑*440m/1445ft* ⏱*2hr 30min*

This route enables you to appreciate the fell's northern aspect and wade Wythop Moss for the fun of it.

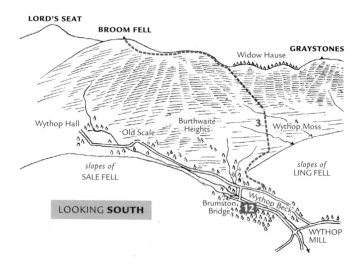

Forest track at junction post 29

3 Walk due south up the road over the beck and turn right at the T-junction to reach the gate close to the track entrance to **Burthwaite Cottage**. The open track quickly comes to a fork, where you swing left with the more regular passage. This follows the fence above Burthwaite. Pass on beyond the red wicket-gate, from where the steep slopes of Ling Fell diminish. Advance to a gate and embark on the long straight crossing of **Wythop Moss**. The route is an old sheep drove, with some evidence of walling, and the path slips through a fence-gate close to the mid-point gill ford. At last the dry banks beneath **Widow Hause** are reached. Step over a quad track and ascend half-left to the depression at the eastern end of the plantations in Widow Hause. Join the ridge path and follow this east. After an early rise the winding trail makes easy progress to a final rise to the landmark cairn.

The summit

A fine currick has been raised in recent years next to a more ragged shelter, adding a certain gravitas to this summit and encouraging visitors to tarry a little longer. The view is divided between the maritime realm of the greater Solway beyond Maryport and inner Lakeland – a pleasing prospect to peruse.

Summit cairn and wind-break, with Lord's Seat behind

Safe descent

The swiftest line in poor weather is to head W down the ridge and then S (**2**) through the forestry back to Darling How.

Ridge routes

Lord's Seat →*1.6km/1 mile* ↓*30m/100ft* ↑*70m/230ft* ⏱*30min*
Cross the fence-stile and follow the winding grassy trod along the ridge, swinging from E to SE on the climb to the cairnless top.

Graystones →*2.4km/1½ miles* ↓*140m/460ft* ↑*85m/280ft* ⏱*40min*
Head W, following the obvious path. This naturally angles with the spine of the ridge SW then W down to the depression, where the wall bounding the forest edge is followed over the intermediate knoll. At the second depression cross the fence-stile and rise S to the small cairn on Graystones.

9 CARL SIDE 746M/2448FT

Climb it from	Millbeck **6**, Old Sawmill Tearoom **17** or High Side **19**
Character	Domed top of the Ullock Pike ridge and no mean viewpoint
Fell-friendly route	5
Summit grid ref	NY 255 281
Link it with	Dodd, Long Side or Skiddaw
Part of	The Skiddaw Skyline

The sleek lines of Carl Side when viewed from the Keswick vale accord with its position at the southwestern shoulder of Skiddaw. It forms the fulcrum to the Ullock Pike ridge, with the point of connection, Carlside Col, sitting at the head of two deep glens. To the northwest, Southerndale is the perfect place for the solace-seeking fellwanderer. To the southeast, the claustrophobic valley of Slades Beck was once the regular line of ascent for Skiddaw. Yet it is between the ravines of Slades and Doups that the most eye-catching feature is found: the abrupt ridge of Carsleddam. Completely smothered in a dense cloak of heather, this lower arm of the fell is seldom climbed – even sheep give it a miss. In fact, so few walkers come this way that, for all the quality of the summit's setting, no cairn has been raised.

↑ *The distinctive shape of Carl Side, enveloping Carsleddam, seen from the south* 81

There are several other approaches to choose from in addition to Southerndale (6) and Slades Beck (4). A clutch of other options (1–3) start from the south at Millbeck and there is a straightforward, shady, graded ascent to enjoy from the Sawmill Tearoom too (5).

Ascent from Millbeck 6

Direct →2km/1¼ miles ↑610m/2000ft ⏲1hr 50min

The direct line from the south

1 Take a footpath, signed 'Skiddaw', departing from the access lane to the exotic Ben-y-Craig and follow on up a confined passage through kissing-gates. On emerging, advance to where a turf-carpet path sweeps left up the fell, uninhibited by bracken. Cross a fence-stile en route to the first high brow and there go through a broken wall and head up by **White Stones**, an intriguing large outcrop of quartz. The path has been engineered with water grips to protect it from wash-out and slants up the heather slope to the summit.

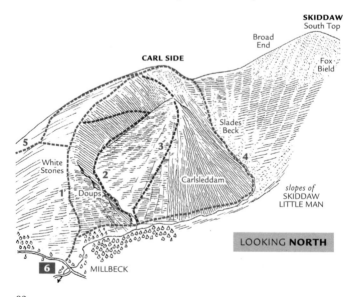

Via Doups →2.5km/1½ miles ↑615m/2020ft ⏱2hr 15min

A more inventive route, for walkers who love to delve

2 Set out with Route **1** but keep forward with the path as towards the Slades Beck valley, but after crossing a fence-stile bear left to follow the gill underneath **Doups** up on the south bank on an intermittent sheep trod. Pass

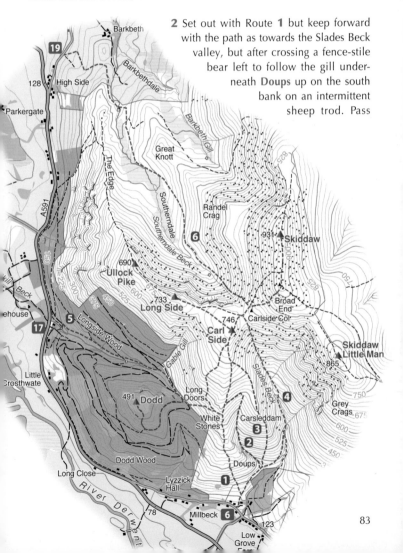

83

under the outcropping to reach a small mine cave and the scant remains of a bothy. Keep on upward along the gill into the heather, using a lateral sheep track to cut left to connect with the main ridge ascent and turn right to the summit.

Via Carsleddam →*2.3km/1½ miles* ↑*610m/2005ft* ⏲*2hr 20min*

The prominent ridge of Carsleddam looks far too good to miss but, with an abundance of heather and no hint of a path, this one's only for pioneers brimming with energy.

3 Set out with Route **2** but, at the gill between **Doups** and Carsleddam, step over to start finding your own line north through the bracken and then the dense heather. After what may seem like an interminable tussle, with little hint of even a lateral sheep trod, the ridge narrows and modest outcropping gives character and form to the fell. Keep to the crest to find the first heather-free moment on the very top of **Carsleddam**. The ridge descends a little then mounts at an easier angle than before, and the heather is less troublesome too. Duly join the direct path slanting right to the summit.

Carsleddam from the summit

Via Slades Beck →2.7km/1¾ miles ↑615m/2020ft ⊕2hr 10min

Once a popular route up Skiddaw, few use this approach today – and wisely so, as the upper reaches are unstable and toilsome.

4 Follow Route **2** to the gill and continue on with the confident path leading beneath Carsleddam. After the weir follow an airy line over outcropping above the ravine. Some distance after passing a lone larch tree the path fords the beck and continues up the deep V-shaped valley, finding little cheer on the loose-stoned pull to the col. The path keeps generally to the right in the final stages, and the grassy end is a blessed relief! Turn left by seasonal Carlside Tarn to complete the ascent with the regular ridge path.

Ascent from Old Sawmill Tearoom 17

Via Skill Beck →3km/2 miles ↑610m/2000ft ⊕2hr

The graded, beckside route to Long Doors col and beyond, on clear paths

5 Cross the footbridge behind the café and follow the metalled roadway up the valley, which homes in on the **Long Doors** col at the top of the valley. Cross the fence-stile on the left and follow the rough path as it climbs to a lateral path. Here either turn left and follow the informal path which climbs the grassy southern slope, or go right to reach the **White Stones** quartz outcrop to join Route **1**, climbing the edge overlooking Doups Gill.

Ascent from High Side 19

Via Southerndale →4.3km/2¾ miles ↑615m/2010ft ⊕2hr 30min

A remote valley approach with a sting in the tail

6 Go through the gate and bear half-left with the track, rising beside the gorse. Where this ends bend right beside the old hedge-line, and where this in turn ends follow the trace of a track that switches up left to a gate then traverses a field to a gate/ladder-stile. The green track comes over the ridge pasture and swings right above **Southerndale Beck**. Pass on along the shelf

Frozen tarn in Carlside Col (photo: Andrew Locking)

via a gate. The track duly crosses a broad plank-bridge over the beck, beside a twin-roomed sheepfold. Once up the worn nearby bank, bend right on a grass track which improves as it advances up **Southerndale**, keeping well above the marshy dale bottom. As the dale comes to its inevitable headwall the path, a redundant shepherds' drove, peters out, and you face the final panting climb, pathless, to the col. At the top go right to reach the summit.

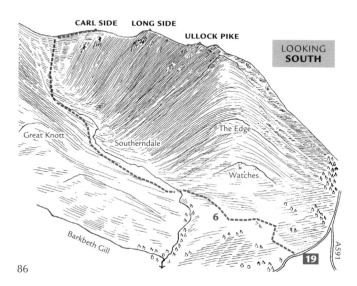

The summit

A loosely assembled cairn rests on the shallow domed summit beside the trade route from Millbeck to Skiddaw. The best viewpoint is a short distance south. Here you can sit and peer over the edge down over Carsleddam towards the Keswick vale and the grand array of fells surrounding Derwentwater.

Safe descents

The best recourse in poor weather is down the regular path S (**1**) for Millbeck. For a sheltered route to destinations above Bassenthwaite, head NE (**6**). The steep descent from the col NW into Southerndale works very well – better than the usual way down the Ullock Pike ridge.

Ridge routes

Dodd →*2.1km/1¼ mile* ↓*360m/1185ft* ↑*115m/380ft* ⏲*40min*
Head S down the main path ultimately destined for Millbeck. On reaching the prominent quartz outcrop of White Stones break right on a path which soon dips down a steep rough slope to a fence-stile accessing the Long Doors col. Join the forest track W, which becomes a path, climbing naturally to the summit.

Long Side →*0.7km/½ mile* ↓*35m/115ft* ↑*40m/130ft* ⏲*15min*
Walk NW and a path is evident – more so when you come to the northern edge and unite with the regular ridge path, which makes the gentle rise to the small cairn on the summit.

Skiddaw →*1.3km/¾ mile* ↓*30m/100ft* ↑*210m/695ft* ⏲*45min*
Head NNE, descending to Carlside Col, with the shallow pool to the right. The path cannot be in doubt as it forges a way NE up the steep slatey slope. By far the more agreeable line is to stick assiduously to the true ridge, branching slightly right early on to wind up the prow of Broad End. By either route the slippery slate means you must watch every step. Don't rush. The horizon gained, simply follow the spine of the ridge due N to the summit column.

10 CARROCK FELL 662M/2172FT

Climb it from	Mosedale **33**, Stone Ends **32**, Carrock Beck **31** or Grainsgill Bridge **34**
Character	A remarkable rocky top once circled by stone ramparts
Fell-friendly route	5
Summit grid ref	NY 342 336
Link it with	High Pike
Part of	The Northern Crown

Quite unlike any of its near neighbours, the complex geological structure of Carrock Fell adds greatly to its appeal. One component is gabbro, an anti-magnetic volcanic rock which can send a compass needle haywire. The volcanic exposures are also more evident on this fell than on any other in the Northern Fells. Climbers will encounter the large boulders beneath Snail Shell Crag – the largest, shaped like a small house, known as the Chapel Stone.

The greatest enigma lies on the summit. Oval in plan, the stone ramparts that girdle the felltop have never been excavated so their origin is obscure. The felltop might have been a place of pilgrimage in an ancient landscape, rather than a place of retreat in times of threat, and the 'ramparts' may instead be a rock necklace defining 'hallowed ground'. The fell certainly sits at a strategic location, overlooking the vast lowlands of the Eden and Solway.

↑ *Carrock Fell from the east at Hutton Roof*

There's a wide range of routes to choose from here, from the direct route through the single chink in the armour of the eastern escarpment on Rake Trod (3) to the circuitous approaches from the west via Miton Hill (6–7), including two contrasting routes from the north (4–5) and from the south (1–2).

Ascent from Mosedale 33

Direct →2.3km/1½ miles ↑430m/1415ft ⊕1hr 20min

A steep heather-challenged ascent, rewarded with views into the Caldew valley

Secreted fold to the right of Route 1

1 Step up off the road opposite the green-doored barn of Mosedale House. Head straight up the bracken-and-gorse fellside from the wall-end on a tangible path. The path switches left to pass a lone rowan, then works on up, with heather and boulders, keeping to the right of a dense area of

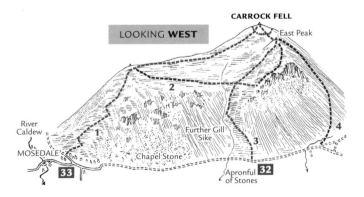

gorse, along the top of boulder scree, to arrive at a low crescent bield (shelter) on a shelf.

Large sheepfold built with stones from ancient ramparts

Pass on over this shelf, climbing through the heather to a far more substantial bield with complete walls. The path beats a way through the increasingly dense heather to reach the fell brow. The temptation to visit the viewpoint cairn, commanding a fine view into the Caldew valley, is difficult to resist. Backtrack to be sure of relocating the path. Follow the consistent path on north-west as it crosses the moorland. There is the odd rock and marshy patch before the ultimate rise to the large sheepfold. Trend left to come alongside the stone rampart and reach the summit cairn.

Via the eastern edge →2.6km/1½ miles ↑460m/1510ft
⏱1hr 20min

A grand little adventure for a sunny day, with little in the way of a path early on or near the end

2 Follow Route **1** to the brink of the plateau but branch right just before the cairn on the first brow. Aim across a pooled hollow to a second small cairn, and trend northwest then north to locate a curious sheepfold clinging to a low east-facing crag. Keep on north to reach a path which leads to the top of the **Further Gill Sike** gully. Ignore the popular shepherds' path but contour on through the heather with a beaten path. Pass a cairn and reach the edge, overlooking the declivity of **the Trough**. Now turn up the slope, without further hint of a path, and climb through the heather, over boulders interspersed with low juniper, to reach the **east peak**. Continue west on the main ridge path to the summit.

Ascent from Stone Ends 32

Via Rake Trod →1.6km/1 mile ↑420m/1380ft ◷1hr

The well-worn direct approach from the east

3 From the open road go to the right of the shallow quarry, quickly picking up the rising path which slants diagonally across the fellside. Keep to the older zig-zags – descending walkers have worn a newer way along the scree margin. The path becomes easier as it comes above a prominent rowan rooted in a projecting rock. Here it heads up the gully from **Further Gill Sike**, with

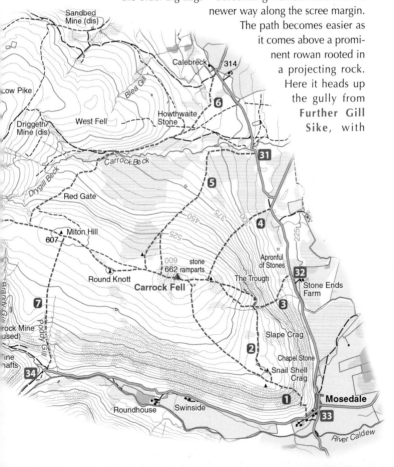

two pines prominent up to the right amid the heather. The path is stepped and ends as a narrow eroded trench, with heather at armpit level. Step onto the heather moor, heading up past a small sheepfold – a throne of sorts, with a gather wall. The path continues through the heather, stepping over the natural rocky barrier to reach the **east peak**, with its diminutive cairn and simply massive eastward view. The true summit lies a short distance west.

Via the common above Linewath →*1.6km/1 mile* ↑*420m/1370ft* ⏱*1hr*

A pathless pant straight to the summit, which would make a good descent paired with Route 3

4 Walk up the road about half a kilometre to where it bends right. Cross the close-cropped common to a few gorse bushes. Here ford a tiny gill and face the bank of bracken with confidence. The fern 'skirt' is quickly overcome, although there is no hint of a path, other than that created by sheep. Continue up the slope, with sphagnum and grass and the odd boulder. Keep rising, initially holding a right-hand bias to avoid the rocky escarpment. At the top you should arrive at the **east peak**, but there are no hazards if you find yourself accidentally drawn to the true summit on a rightward course.

Ascent from Carrock Beck 31

Direct →*2.2km/1½ miles* ↑*400m/1315ft* ⏱*1hr 15min*

A more measured variation which gives a sure path to the top

5 Short of a sheepfold complex, just by the parking spot, pick up a path which rises consistently to the ridge west of the stony summit prow. The steeper left-hand fork, higher up, is the creation of over-eager descending walkers. The better choice is to keep right and enjoy the walk back left to the summit along the ridge.

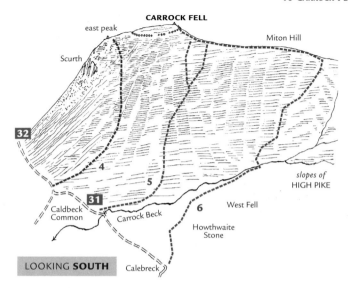

CARROCK FELL

east peak

Scurth

Miton Hill

32

4

5

slopes of
HIGH PIKE

31

Caldbeck
Common

Carrock Beck

6

West Fell

Howthwaite
Stone

LOOKING **SOUTH**

Calebreck

Via Miton Hill →4.7km/3 miles ↑370m/1215ft ⏱2hr

A roundabout and remote approach on a variety of terrain

6 Walk about a kilometre up the road to just short of Calebreck to find an open bridle-track leading west from the roadside. A matter of paces along this a low sign directs left onto a grass path. This lovely turf trail sweeps easily across the open pasture and at one point is only 100 metres from the **Howthwaite Stone**. Converge with a more obvious track as you approach the **Carrock Beck** valley and continue upstream. Soon find a lesser path, forking half-left parallel with the beck, which leads to a ford and an abrupt ascent of the Miton Hill fellside. This becomes a definite hollow-way groove, known as **Red Gate**, which leads up to a saddle on the ridge. Near the top an alternative drove-way, seldom trod, offers a fabulous view back on High Pike worth detouring for. Otherwise, complete the ascent and bear left with the ridge path, passing the cairn on **Miton Hill**. Between this top and the main summit lies an area of damp sphagnum and exposed peat. This can be avoided by visiting the cairn on **Round Knott** and walking on from there to the prominent stony summit.

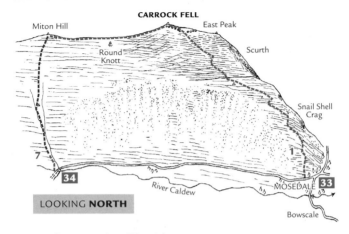

CARROCK FELL

Miton Hill East Peak

Round Knott

Scurth

Snail Shell Crag

1

MOSEDALE 33

34

River Caldew

LOOKING NORTH

Bowscale

Ascent from Grainsgill Bridge 34

Via Poddy Gill → 2.7km/1¾ miles ↑375m/1230ft ⏲2hr

A pathless plod straight up to the ridge

7 Step up north directly from the bridge, cross the tarmac mine road and follow the path through the bracken to ford the gill. Keep to a tangible path

Long view to the fell, on the ridge path from High Pike

up the bank on the left-hand side of the shallow ravine of **Poddy Gill**. As the slope becomes less steep the path vanishes. Keep going uphill, aiming for something that initially looks like a cairn but turns out to be a small bield-wall at the lower end of a rash of boulders, with a large bield over to the right. Maintain your uphill plod, coping with a large expanse of rushes, beyond which grass predominates, onto the marshy ridge to meet the ridge path. Turn east on this, joining Route **6**, to reach the summit.

The summit

Uniquely, the summit cairn is perched not only on a rock plinth, but at the western tip of a remarkable drystone necklace – incomplete, but clearly very ancient indeed. In recent centuries shepherds 'borrowed' some of the stones to construct a now-decrepit sheepfold on the south side. A tour of the ramparts will reveal a few places where some order remains.

Rebuilt summit cairn

The Solway lowlands and Scottish hills sweep round to the north, and the east peak provides the better stance from which to enjoy the exhilarating and extensive eastward prospect over the Caldew and further Eden vales towards the Pennine chain.

Safe descents

To the N tame slopes lead down to the Carrock Beck valley (**5**) for the unenclosed road north of Mosedale. Find the path some 300 metres W of the summit. Otherwise, the wisest option is to follow the Further Gill Sike path (**3**), which leads down from the east peak, to the road at Stone Ends. For a direct route to the hamlet of Mosedale take the tenuous trod heading SE (**1**) through the heather (disconcerting in mist).

Ridge route

High Pike →*3.2km/2 miles* ↓*100m/330ft* ↑*100m/330ft* ⏲*1hr*
Step down through the stony rampart onto the peaty ridge to head W. Beyond Miton Hill skirt the head of Drygill Beck in turning N to reach the summit cairn.

11 DODD 502M/1647FT

Climb it from	Millbeck **6** or Old Sawmill Tearoom **17**
Character	An excellent little viewpoint over Bassenthwaite Lake
Fell-friendly route	7
Summit grid ref	NY 244 273
Link it with	Carl Side

Nature endowed this lowly fell with a relaxed mantle of trees and open pasture. But in the 20th century foresters 'spruced' it up, and as the conifers matured so Dodd became, for a time, a joyless place to wander. Not any more. Since 2001, the crown of misplaced firs has been felled, and the debris of rotting stumps gives myriad beetles, bugs and fungi a happy habitat. Dodd's main tracks have been opened to create handsome walking parades, and unfailingly beautiful outlooks over Bassenthwaite and Derwentwater have been revealed, most notably from the summit.

Also in 2001, the fell's interest was further enhanced by the return of breeding osprey to the shore of Bassenthwaite, the culmination of years of hard work by the Lake District Osprey Project encouraging the migrating birds to nest and breed here. The ospreys have returned every year since, giving visitors good reason to come to the designated viewpoints.

↑ *Dodd from Sale Fell, reflected in Bassenthwaite*

Above the Old Sawmill Tearoom various casual visitor trails begin, utilised here in four different approaches to the summit (4–7) – although only one is the designated 'Dodd Summit Trail'. Three other lines of attack from the south are also described (1–3), including one from Millbeck which manages to stay clear of the forestry as far as Long Doors (1), the col that links Dodd to the lower slopes of Skiddaw.

Ascent from Millbeck 6

Via the head of Doups →*2.2km/1½ miles* ↑*400m/1310ft* ⏱*1hr 15min*

The relatively conifer-free option

1 Follow the confined footpath stepping up by **Ben-y-Craig** and emerge through the top kissing-gate. Stride forward on the obvious green carpet rising half-left through the bracken up the fellside. Part-way up cross a fence-stile, and higher still encounter a cross-wall. At this point leave the regular ascending path, turn left and follow the wall, contouring northwest. Beyond an awkward wall junction the path arrives at a fence-stile as the White Stones route leaves the **Long Doors** col. Step over and follow the forest track right only a

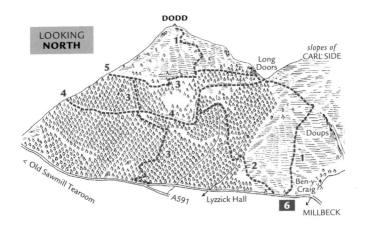

Viewpoint bench near Long Doors

matter of 30 metres before switching acutely left, signed to Dodd summit. A bench at the first corner provides a fine spot to rest before heading on west, with the track climbing easily. Above the conifers join the engineered path winding up right to the summit.

Via Scalebeck Gill →3.5km/2¼ miles ↑415m/1360ft ⏱1hr 30min

A shady way to snake up from the south

2 A footpath is signed off the road at the west end of Millbeck, beside a small layby. Quickly crossing a stile, the path runs through the bracken and rises to clip the top of a larch plantation, then heads up to a fence-stile set into a wall-gap. The path then enters Dodd's dark woodland. Bending left to ford a tiny gill, wind up to enter a green forest ride. Cross this diagonally, guided by the footpath post. Your way is damp underfoot initially, and dark, until you step onto a lateral path, going left to unite with a rising track. Here turn right and rise steadily to reach the **Long Doors** col. Passing the cairn on the col switch acutely left on the rising track to join Route **1**.

Direct →*3.2km/2 miles* ↑*415m/1370ft* ⏱*1hr 20min*

An energetic assault, with many a twist and turn among the trees

3 Walk west along the road from Millbeck about a kilometre to reach the junction with the main road. From the layby here walk across level ground into the wood. Quickly the path switches right and then left as it climbs steadily up through the mature woodland. Coming into the tall trees the path becomes more focused on ascent, making an abrupt beeline straight up the conifer bank to reach a lateral forest track. Turn left with the rock-cut track. When you reach a wide turning area with an open outlook, swing right then immediately left, up the conifer-shaded path. Climb to a lateral path and turn right. This lovely fell path unshackles itself from the shade of the

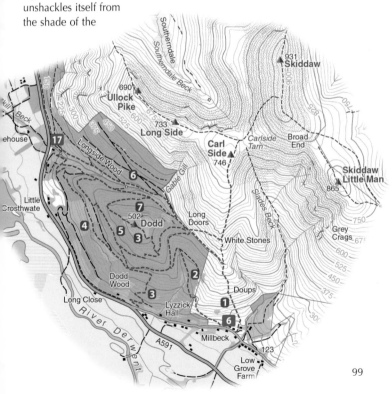

trees as it too takes several twists as it comes up to a dip, with a viewpoint bench to the right and the regular way heading left. The path is quickly joined by the path from Long Doors. Climb the made trail to the summit.

Ascent from Old Sawmill Tearoom 17

Four ways to make use of the forestry tracks from this angle, Route 6 the swiftest and simplest and Route 7 the least frequented, making a perfect ascent route to marry with any of the others in descent

Via the upper osprey viewpoint →3km/2 miles ↑405m/1325ft ⏱1hr 20min
4 Keep to the right of the footbridge and follow a tall sign directing the eager flock of birdwatchers to the two osprey viewpoints. When you arrive at the main track, with the lower viewpoint near right, bear up left and rise to and beyond the upper viewpoint. The track climbs steadily. In due course it comes round the south side of the fell to curve north and reach the **Long Doors** col. Pass round left, following the sign to Dodd Summit, acutely left, with Route **1**.

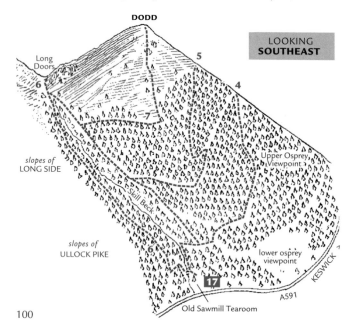

Via the upper west side trail →*2.9km/1¾ miles* ↑*380m/1270ft* ⏱*1hr 15min*
5 Start with Route **4** on the regular path, which rises and bends right to arrive at a minor cross-way, with the lower osprey viewpoint signed ahead. Turn left here, following the forest path which rises to merge with a more substantial track. Continue uphill and take the first track right. This forest track swings round the ridge-end and ascends steadily. Watch for a footpath breaking steeply hard left off the open track. In the lee of the pine, follow this up and contour on a narrow shelf southeast, coming through a conifer tunnel to unite with Route **3**.

Via Skill Beck →*2.7km/1¾ miles* ↑*395m/1295ft* ⏱*1hr 20min*
6 You may choose to head up the left-hand side of the valley (on the true right bank of **Skill Beck**) on a forest track. Cross the footbridge at the bottom of the beck to zig-zag and finally turn up right, with the rising track, to reach the road below the **Long Doors** col. Close to the top of the col follow signs guiding up right for Dodd summit (Route **1**).

Via the northwest ridge →*2.2km/1½ miles* ↑*385m/1255ft* ⏱*1hr 10min*
7 Follow Route **5** but take the second turn off the substantial track that goes up parallel with **Skill Beck**, rather than the first. An acute turn leads onto a seldom-walked green track. This rises, coming along a shelf to end abruptly. (It is possible to slip through the thin conifer fringe ahead to stand on a brink and admire a fabulous view.) Turn up the ridge. A shallow groove starts the ascent to a narrow path which strikes up the felled northwest ridge, with tufts of heather and coarse grasses among the tangle of decaying timber. Two stepped stages of ridge lead to the crest and the summit memorial.

The summit memorial

The summit

An attractive flake of raw slate, standing as a memorial to two members of the 1st Seaton Scout Group, marks the summit. The life of the memorial, like that of the surrounding conifers, will be shorter than that of a standard cairn. What will endure is the view. Scan the southern horizon from the Helvellyn range round by Derwentwater and all those wonderful fells down Borrowdale and of the nearer Northwestern group, with Grisedale Pike the most compelling mountain peak. Wander the short way to the northwest brink for a stunning view over Bassenthwaite Lake.

Safe descents

Follow the made way back SE (**1**), winding down to connect with the forest trails. Then go left (N then NW) for a downward trudge back to the Old Sawmill Tearoom car park (**6** or **7**).

Ridge route

Carl Side →*2.1km/1¼ miles* ↓*115m/380ft* ↑*360m/1185ft* ⏲*1hr 10min*
Dodd is subsidiary to Carl Side, joined at the Long Doors col. Brought together as one climb their summits make a wonderful 'little and large' combination – two points of high elation. Turn back down the graded trail SE, which becomes a track leading gently down N and E to the Long Doors col. Step over the fence-stile in the pass and climb the path ascending the rough slope until it comes up to the quartz outcrop of White Stones. Here join the Millbeck path climbing N to the summit.

Dodd from White Stones on the route to Carl Side

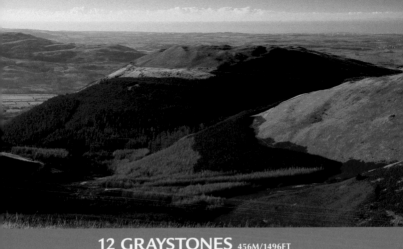

12 GRAYSTONES 456M/1496FT

Climb it from	Harrot Hill Farm **10**, Embleton Church **11**, Brumston Bridge **12** or Spout Force **9**
Character	The grassy end of a fine striding ridge from Lord's Seat
Fell-friendly route	1
Summit grid ref	NY 178 264
Link it with	Broom Fell
Part of	The Aiken Beck Horseshoe

Rising directly east of the village of High Lorton, Graystones forms the western extremity of the Lord's Seat ridge. The felltop has three distinct elements – Kirk Fell, with its wonderful viewpoint cairn, a most rewarding spot from which to survey the Vale of Lorton and the Loweswater Fells; and slightly higher still to the east, two rival tops with less rewarding outlooks. To the north, Wythop Moss defends the fell from walkers unwilling to get their feet wet in pursuit of a wide and unpeopled summit panorama.

Fellow walkers are at a premium here but you have the views and the skylarks to keep you company. The enchanting back lane linking Hundith Hill Road with Armaside Farm carries little more than farm traffic, and the other lanes to the north are not much busier, with winding Whinlatter Pass to the south the busiest thoroughfare by far hereabouts, though that more with cyclists than with motorists.

↑ *Graystones' eastern aspect, seen from Lord's Seat*

Choose from short sharp routes from the Whinlatter Forest side (4–6) and longer, more improvised alternatives from the north and west (1–3). When the buses are running, you could even match them up as a traverse without too much road-walking. But please note that there is no recognised route direct from the village of High Lorton.

Ascent from Harrot Hill Farm 10

Via Kirk Fell →4.4km/2¾ miles ↑365m/1200ft
🕐1hr 15min

In terms of gradient, probably the easiest ascent in the book

1 At Harrot Hill Farm a footpath sign directs off the road through the gated barns. The track leads on by further gates. Ignore the branch right to the mast and instead keep ahead via a gate by young hedges on the rise of **Harrot**. The open track veers across a field to become a green-way, sloping up beside the line of beech trees to reach a stile.

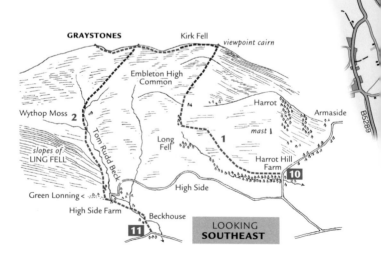

LOOKING **SOUTHEAST**

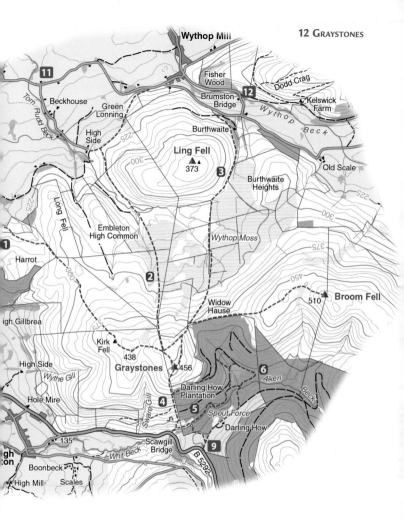

A clear path leads on and, where the gorse ends, with an old boundary bank visible, bear half-right, with only sheep paths in the open pasture, aiming to the right of the skyline hilltop, where you will find a fence-stile. The direct route keeps to the high ground southeast but it is worth bearing slightly to the right, pathlessly, towards the viewpoint cairn on the western brink of Kirk Fell.

Cross the grassy top of **Kirk Fell**, marked by two stones. Keep northeast to join up with the direct route, which becomes a more evident path as it crosses a depression and then climbs onto a subsidiary top. Go through the wall-gap and bend half-right on the path, which dips and rises to the summit cairn.

Ascent from Embleton Church 11

Both these routes could also be tackled from Wythop Mill/Brumston Bridge, which is linked to the lane end south of Embleton Church by a green lane aptly named Green Lonning.

Via Tom Rudd Beck →4km/2½ miles ↑365m/1200ft ⏱1hr 20min

2 Follow the private road directly opposite the layby, signed 'High Side'. The gated lane leads up by several lovely beckside dwellings to arrive at the barns of **High Side Farm**, with the white-washed farmhouse up to the left. Pass on through the gate and bear uphill with the green lane (**Green Lonning**). Find a footpath signed right at a gate to 'Embleton High Common'. The path follows a hedge beneath a bank of gorse to join an open track. Follow this through a gate, and where the track forks keep right to a fording point in **Tom Rudd Beck**. When the tracks splits in two, take the left-hand option rising directly ahead (south-southeast). The track quickly dwindles and is lost, but this line avoids the bracken and gives a view of three old larch trees on the far bank. Go through a metal gate and continue south. The going is potentially damp through the rushes, with several old drainage trenches to cross. Pass the foundations of a wall by the merest trace of an old reservoir before the slope steepens. Ascend the mossy slope to come beside the rising fence/old wall and arrive at a hurdle-gate, which has to be crossed carefully. Keep up the rushy bank alongside the old wall and pass above a massive stone, where two field boundaries converge on the far side, to cross an old wall/fence and complete the climb. The grassy ridge path is met and followed left across a shallow hollow to the summit.

Via Wythop Moss →6km/3¾ miles ↑350m/1150ft ⏱1hr 40min

3 Follow Route **1** as far as Green Lonning and then follow the green-way to its end to join the road through Wythop Mill, taking the first right fork. Walk along this to a gate set to the acute right before the access drive to Burthwaite Cottage. The open track quickly comes to a fork, where you swing left with

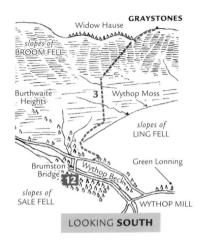

GRAYSTONES

Widow Hause

slopes of
BROOM FELL

Burthwaite
Heights

Wythop Moss

3

slopes of
LING FELL

Green Lonning

Brumston
Bridge

Wythop Beck

12

slopes of
SALE FELL

WYTHOP MILL

LOOKING **SOUTH**

the more regular passage. This follows the fence above **Burthwaite**. Pass on beyond the red wicket-gate, from where the steep slopes of Ling Fell diminish. Advance to a gate and embark on the long straight crossing of **Wythop Moss**. The route is an old sheep drove, with some evidence of walling, and the path slips through a fence-gate close to the mid-point gill ford. At last (and with great relief) reach the dry banks beneath **Widow Hause**. Step over a quad track and ascend half-right to the dip in the ridge to the right of the Widow Hause plantation. Clamber over the fence-stile and follow the path up the bank in a southwesterly direction to reach the summit cairn.

Looking east across Widow Hause

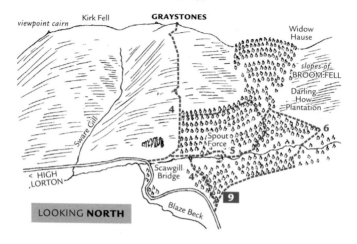

Ascent from Spout Force 9

Via Scawgill Bridge →*1.6km/1 mile* ↑*295m/970ft* ⏱*1hr*

4 Descend directly from the first parking area (coming from Keswick) on a path that slips down the bank and over the **Aiken Beck** footbridge. Turn left, passing through a hand-gate, short of **Scawgill Bridge** (you can also park at the bridge and connect with the route via the adjacent hand-gate). After some 30 metres find a path that switches acutely right up through the gorse and loose slate debris to accompany the steep forest-bounding wall. The slope eases, thankfully, above the brief rock-step, and the path slips through the broken wall to reach the summit. How quick was that?

Via Spout Force →*2km/1¼ miles* ↑*305m/1000ft* ⏱*1hr 10min*

An interesting alternative approach on forest tracks which includes an intimate view over the Spout Force ravine – the second variant having the simpler start

5 As with Route **4**, descend to cross the **Aiken Beck** footbridge, but this time turn upstream. The embowered path includes steps, and a spur brings the questing walker to a little viewing platform where the picturesque **Spout Force** is seen to advantage. Step back and then continue in confined circumstances

108

tight beside a defending fence above the ravine. The path dips down to the beckside, but does not cross it. Instead keep up through the scrubby stumps and young conifers entwined with the odd bramble and fallen limb to come up into the mature forest and duly join the forest track. Turn right and, at the track fork, bear left away from the beck. Ascend with the main track up the re-entrant valley and at the second junction swing sharp left on the forest track. Where this track then hairpins right, keep forward on a confined path, somewhat hemmed in by conifers, on a heather-lined path which opens on a cut shelf leading to the forest-bounding fence and broken wall. Step over and join Route **4** as you climb the comparatively short, steep slope beside the broken wall, scramble up the rock-step and keep ascending, finally bearing right to the summit.

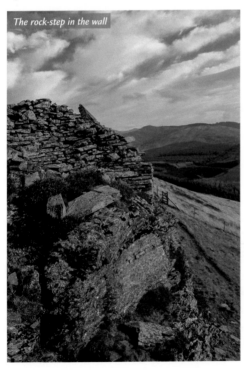

The rock-step in the wall

6 From the first parking area (coming from Keswick) follow the open forestry track, passing the barrier close to Darling How Farm. As the track gently descends watch to bear left with the forest track which then goes right to cross Aiken Beck bridge then shortly switches left. At the next fork go left and then, after crossing the gill, bear up right on a rougher forest track. This arrives at a track intersection, the slope ahead felled in 2018. Swing left on the forest track to join Route **5** to the summit.

The summit

Two high points vie for top billing, dissected by the broken ridge-crossing wall. The cairn to the east seems the natural summit, although the top on the west side is a better place to stand. The views are unremarkable, but there is plenty to study on the maritime front, and both the Aiken Beck and Hobcarton valleys are clearly visible.

Safe descents

The path beside the broken wall leading due S (**4**) brings you swiftly to Scawgill Bridge down a steep grassy path which can be troublesome when wet or icy. In other directions the ground is less steep but the journey much longer. Route **1** (NW) via Kirk Fell is entirely on firm ground, whereas Routes **2** (N) and **3** (NE) encounter Wythop Moss.

Ridge route

Broom Fell →*2.4km/1½ miles* ↓*85m/280ft* ↑*140m/460ft* ⏱*30min*
A simple matter. Descend NNE to a fence-stile and follow the edge of the Darling How Plantation over the Widow Hause ridge. At the end of the forest edge ascend the open bank onto the fell and follow a clear path all the way, curving SE to reach the handsome summit cairn.

Broom Fell and Lord's Seat from the summit

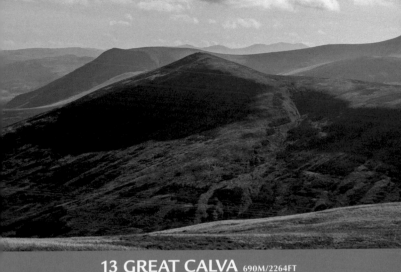

13 GREAT CALVA 690M/2264FT

Climb it from	Skiddaw House **21**, Peter House **20**, Horsemoor Hills **22** or Grainsgill Bridge **34**
Character	Heathery hill fleetingly seen from the A66 through the Glenderaterra Gap
Fell-friendly route	3
Summit grid ref	NY 291 312
Link it with	Knott
Part of	The Northern Crown

Travellers on the A66 sweeping west from Threlkeld catch a tantalising glimpse of a low peak through the Glenderaterra gap and no doubt wonder what lies beyond. This is Great Calva, right at the heart of Skiddaw Forest, a peaceful tract of fell country otherwise known as the Back o'Skidda. Also central to a beautiful swathe of heather moor, which begins on Little Calva and spills down a trio of ridges to the east of Knott – Snab, Cocklakes and Coomb Height – it draws the eye of many a visitor to the Skiddaw House independent hostel too.

While the main summit ridge is a dry spine of rock, the more junior ridge of Little Calva to the west is less blessed, being a mix of morass and heather. However, this aspect lays claim to Whitewater Dash, or Dash Falls, one of the most thrilling and graceful of Lakeland waterfalls.

↑ *Great Calva, with Lonscale Fell behind to the left, from Knott*   111

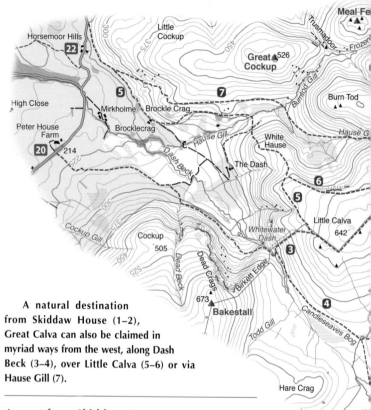

A natural destination from Skiddaw House (1–2), Great Calva can also be claimed in myriad ways from the west, along Dash Beck (3–4), over Little Calva (5–6) or via Hause Gill (7).

Ascent from Skiddaw House 21

Two straightforward routes from the hostel, Route 2 the better for ascent if you choose to combine them

Via the south ridge →*2.4km/1½ miles* ↑*250m/820ft* ⏱*1hr 10min*
1 Follow the supply track which leads northwest to a footbridge and then ford the first vigorous splashes of the **River Caldew**. Continue until the slope takes off and then leave the track and rise through the heather up the slopes as they taper towards the south ridge to reach the conical **south top**. Pass on by the cairn and follow the ridge-top fence to the summit at the left-hand angle of the fence.

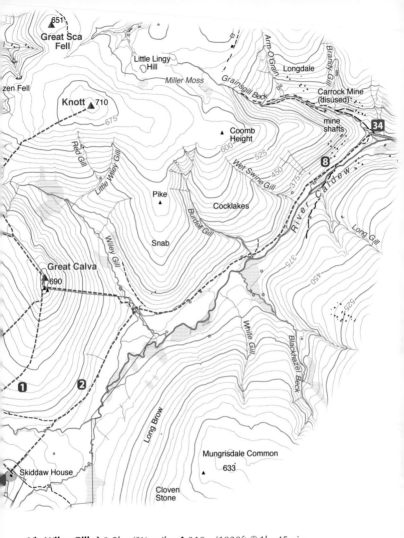

Via Wiley Gill →3.5km/2¼ miles ↑310m/1020ft ⊕1hr 45min

2 A wet path heads northeast from Skiddaw House, crossing the **River Caldew** by a footbridge. From here keep to the green trod now running along the base of Great Calva's heather moor. When you reach a circular sheepfold bear left

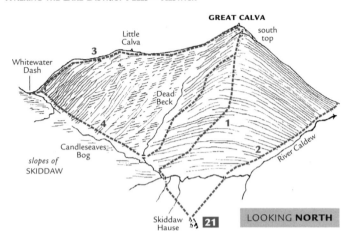

with the meandering **Wiley Gill**, on its west bank, watching for a path that slips up a gully in the steep flanking slope to climb into the tangle of heather. This duly bends right to reach and go through a hand-gate in the fence. Climb close to the fence direct to the **south top**, and here cross the fence by the wooden railings to reach the summit.

Ascent from Peter House 20

Via Whitewater Dash and Little Calva →5.5km/3½ miles ↑495m/1625ft ⏱2hr 15min

The most popular line from the west

3 Follow the open road, through gates, and fork right from the tarmac access road, where the bridle-track (and supply road for Skiddaw House) begins. (There is no access across the Dash valley via the farm road.) The track leads on through another gate to rise up the impressive valley head beneath **Dead Crags** to reach the top of **Whitewater Dash** (Dash Falls). Go through the gate and follow the track over the culverted bridge, then leave the track at the sharp right-hand bend. A path contours left then sets to work climbing the tough heather slope close to the fence. As the slope eases the path drifts right,

Dash Falls from the Skiddaw House supply road

following a gully to come onto the plateau and regain contact with the fence. Follow this over marshy ground as it turns northeast by the top of **Little Calva**, and from there the fence and path head up to the main summit.

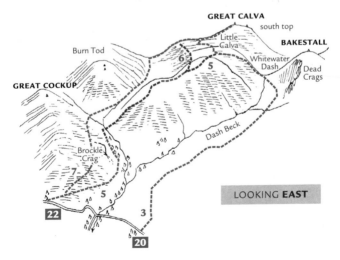

LOOKING **EAST**

Via Candleseaves Bog →*5.7km/3½ miles* ↑*490m/1610ft* ⏱*2hr 10min*
4 Set out with Route **3** but continue on the supply track from above **Whitewater Dash** until a lonely hawthorn bush is reached, where **Dead Beck** runs under the track. Branch off on the south side of the beck and follow the very evident path which skirts to the right of the marshy hollow and soon embarks on a steady northeastwards ascent. Coming onto drier ground, the path unites with Route **1** to complete the climb left, via the **south top**.

Ascent from Horsemoor Hills 22

Via White Hause →*6.1km/3¾ miles* ↑*510m/1680ft* ⏱*20min*

Two more exploratory approaches over Little Calva

5 Walk north to the gated bridle-track signposted 'Burn Tod'. This leads on unenclosed, providing access for **Brocklecrag** and farm access beyond. As the track approaches a padlocked gate bear left beside the rising wall and beneath the striking outcrop of **Brockle Crag**, with its prominent veins of quartz. The trace of a path rises up a little from the wall to go through a patch of rushes before levelling above the larch copse. The vestige of a path is lost as you come over the bank beyond the copse and cross the line of a green-way above the barn. Walk over the rush marsh to come down to **Hause Gill**, hopping over as best you can manage above the intake wall. Now head up the slope ahead, ignoring the lateral quad track and aiming left of the scree and outcropping for the skyline of the ridge. This brings you onto the top of **White Hause**, a grand little vantage point. Keep to the high ground, finding the trace of a path leading up onto the higher ridge of **Little Calva**. Go south over heathery moor to reach the fence, finding a stile 30 metres from the corner, and from there join the regular path from the top of Whitewater Dash (Route **3**). **6** Alternatively, on reaching the higher ridge of Little Calva, curve east with the scarp above the Hause Gill combe to join the ridge path from Knott, trending southeast to the fence-stile on the ridge where you join Route **3**.

Via Hause Gill →*5.8km/3½ miles* ↑*515m/1685ft* ⏱*2hr*

A consistently good path all the way from the road to the ridge

7 Start out on the Brocklecrag farm track with Route **5** but soon take the sign-posted bridleway rising left (southeast) as a green path. This comes over the broad shoulder above **Brockle Crag** and heads on as a comparatively level track along the southern slopes of Great Cockup, duly drifting downward to ford **Burntod Gill**. Tackle marshy patches as you proceed up the **Hause Gill** valley, becoming very intimate with it in its upper ravine, to emerge onto the ridge at the grassy saddle. Join the ridge path as it rises in a southerly arc to reach the ridge fence and stile where you unite with Route **3**.

Ascent from Grainsgill Bridge 34

Along the River Caldew →4.7km/3 miles ↑400m/1315ft ⊕2hr 15min

Enjoy the free riverside striding before claiming your fell.

8 Cross the bridge and follow the track up the **River Caldew** valley for about 3km. Cross a fence-stile and the subsequent footbridge spanning **Wiley Gill**, beside a large circular sheepfold. Here turn right off the main valley track as it slants up the bank, joining Route **2**.

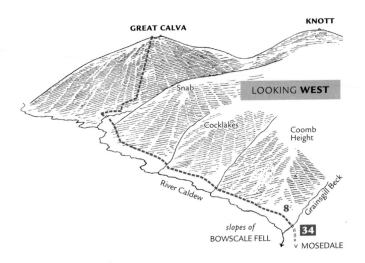

The summit

The fence binds the cairns at either end of the short stony ridge – but may bar your way if you want to use the snug shelter on the east side of the ridge tight below the summit cairn. The lower south top is the better viewpoint and has a handy shelter, facing the view – a long vista through the natural trough through the Cumbrian mountains that is the Glenderaterra gap. Beyond are Thirlmere and Dunmail Raise far to the south – on a clear day you might even see Gummer's How at the southern end of Windermere!

Safe descents

The easiest route is S (**1**), following the path, which in its later stages bends SW to join the Skiddaw House supply track. From here continue S to the hostel or turn right to follow the track back NW to the Dash valley and Peter House.

Ridge route

Knott →2.6km/1½ miles ↓135m/445ft ↑160m/525ft ⏱45min
The steady path makes progress straightforward, even in mist. Leave the north top (the summit), following the path NW down by the fence to cross the stile. The path slants down the fellside to merge with a path from Little Calva. Curve NE through the saddle at the head of the Wiley Gill valley to climb up the grassy slope to the summit cairn on the broad plateau.

Looking to Blencathra from the summit cairn

14 GREAT COCKUP 526M/1726FT

Climb it from	Horsemoor Hills **22** or Longlands **26**
Character	Once a grouse moor but now a quiet pasture flanking secretive Trusmadoor
Fell-friendly route	1
Summit grid ref	NY 273 333
Link it with	Meal Fell

Lying right in the middle of the Uldale Fells, Great Cockup is the extended western arm of a dwindling ridge springing from Great Sca Fell, separated from Meal Fell by the gap of Trusmadoor. This magical ravine was created by glacial melt-water, likely as a result of an ice blockage in Burntod Gill. It harbours the headwaters of the River Ellen, which runs north then west from here, taking in the overspill of Over Water, to the Irish Sea at Maryport.

Like those of its neighbours, the southern slopes are richly adorned with heather, and the remains of redundant stone-walled shooting butts lie on the lower ridge west of the summit. The winding fellside road below Orthwaite Bank passes a gem of a farmhouse, the rose-madder-painted Orthwaite Hall. The original house dated from the late 16th century, while the date-stone on the barn shows 1675 and the initials of the owners at the time, the Richmond family.

↑ *Great Cockup from Stockdale*

You can take this little top from any angle. Most approaches are short and start in the west from Horsemoor Hills (1–4). For a longer but just as natural line direct to scenic Trusmadoor, start from Longlands in the north (5).

Ascent from Horsemoor Hills 22

Via Brockle Crag →*3.3km/2 miles* ↑*320m/1050ft* ⏱*1hr 15min*

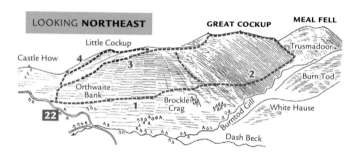

Pick your paths to work your way up from the south.

1 Walk north to the gated bridle-track signposted 'Burn Tod'. This leads on unenclosed, providing access for **Brocklecrag** and farm access beyond. Follow this to the low farm track, turning off 100 metres after the second quarry, on a lovely turf trail. This rises onto the little eminence with a quartz rock rib, and lower down Brockle Crag is noted for its large speckled exposure of quartz. The path contours to the next shoulder. Here bend sharp left with the quad track, up through the heather, to the walled butt. Turn right and continue, passing over a line of broken butts and rising onto the west top, where there is a large cairn. The grassy ridge continues to a smaller cairn marking the summit of the fell. **2** Alternatively, instead of turning directly up the slope, take a less-than-obvious path bending left from the main turf trail. Wade through the bracken and find a strong sheep path contouring through the heather up the Burn Tod valley to reach **Trusmadoor**. Here cut back left up the edge to complete the climb.

Quartz outcropping on top of Brockle Crag

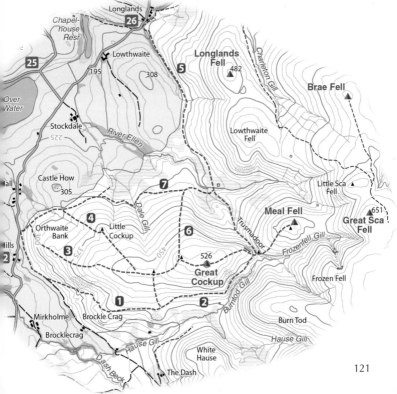

Via Orthwaite Bank →*2.6km/1½ miles* ↑*305m/1000ft* ⏱*1hr 10min*

A less-travelled line of attack

3 Walk north up the road to the bridle-track. From the gate turn abruptly up beside the intake wall on a quad track. As the slope eases find a path branching right, off the quad track, up the fell edge. Frequented more often by sheep than by walkers, this initially beats a path through the bracken as it rises up **Orthwaite Bank**.

Old shooting butt on the ridge

The path dissolves up the blank slope until the fell levels, at which point a more consistent path is found leading by the circular remains of a grouse-shooting butt on the ridge. Follow this path to the summit.

Via Little Cockup →*2.8km/1¾ miles* ↑*310m/1015ft* ⏱*1hr 15min*

A variant visiting the cairn on lowly Little Cockup

4 Start with Route **3** but keep on the quad track direct from the gate (northeast) and, after crossing a marshy patch, rise up a faint path southeast to the knoll of **Little Cockup**, with its neat cairned summit. Beat up through the bracken to reach it and traverse (southeast) pathlessly to join the main ridge path. Coming through the last of the heather, by several ruined butts, the ridge makes one step up to arrive at a cairn on the western end of the summit ridge. This is a great viewpoint in its own right. From here stride on east with Route **1** to the modest summit cairn.

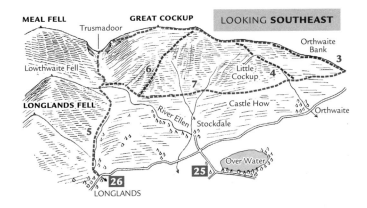

Ascent from Longlands 26

Make a beeline for the bottom of Trusmadoor then take your pick – Route 5 is the steepest and Route 7 the gentlest and most indirect.

Via Trusmadoor →3.5km/2¼ miles ↑320m/1050ft ⏱1hr 25min
5 Go through the gate beside the beck and at once bear right off the green track. Ford Longlands Beck and follow on, taking a track that leads south, close beside a wall. Pass below the spoil of a gated mine-level, and after a ruined shed proceed along the green track to ford the infant **River Ellen**. Three routes fan from this damp dale bottom. For Trusmadoor follow the path as it leads up beside the esker (glacial ridge) to draw through the pass, as neat a place for an ambush as can be conceived. At the southern end, beyond the cairn, cut back up the right-hand edge to gain the summit plateau due west (with Route **2**).

Via northern slopes →5.8km/3½ miles ↑380m/1250ft ⏱1hr 45min
6 Follow Route **5** as far as the ford of the River Ellen, cross the beck to tackle the mire west of the ford and then turn directly south to make your way unproblematically, if tediously, up the pathless north slope. **7** Alternatively, from the ford of the River Ellen, cross the beck and the marsh and find a fell track running round to **Orthwaite Bank** along the northern slopes. Choose from Route **4** via Little Cockup or Route **3** via Orthwaite Bank to reach the summit.

123

The summit

The small cairn is as much as may be expected in this field of grass. The northerly view is extensive towards the Solway lowlands. The near surround of fells is not exciting, although Skiddaw rises imperiously to the south above Bakestall.

Safe descents

The only potential pitfall in mist is the east brink overlooking Trusmadoor. It is best to follow the ridge either E to Trusmadoor (keeping to the clear path south of the edge) or W, turning down S at the stone grouse butt to join the bridleway leading W above Brockle Crag (**1**).

Ridge route

Meal Fell → 1.2km/¾ mile ↓85m/280ft ↑110m/360ft ⊕30min
Walk ENE to the top of Trusmadoor, following the edge down right to the cairn in the pass. Go straight on, climbing NE to the summit shelter.

Brockle Crag

15 GREAT SCA FELL 651M/2136FT

Climb it from	Longlands **26**, Greenhead **27** or Fell Side **28**
Character	A lovely scarp and meeting point of the most northerly ridges above Knott
Fell-friendly route	2
Summit grid ref	NY 291 339
Link it with	Brae Fell, Knott, Longlands Fell or Meal Fell

Sitting at the apex of the Uldale Fells on the northwestern perimeter of Lakeland, the sleek sheep pastures of Great Sca Fell are nothing like the rugged heights of its more famous namesake. But the twin-scarp headlands of Little and Great Sca Fell, best seen from near-western perspectives, have a stirring dignity all their own. Similarly reminiscent of the Howgills is the northeastern ridge of Yard Steel, which rises purposefully out of the Dale Beck valley to join them. Of these three cairned tops the most popular is Little Sca Fell, with its unimpeded northward views.

When Alfred Wainwright researched his guide here back in 1961, he commented on the dedicated life of shepherd Pearson Dalton. Twice weekly Pearson would make the journey on foot from his home in Fell Side to Skiddaw House to tend his flock grazing the wilds of Skiddaw Forest – no quad bikes then… and precious few recreational walkers either!

↑ *Great and Little Sca Fells from Meal Fell*

The fell is usually climbed from one of three little farming hamlets strung along the northern edge of the base of the common, Longlands (1–2), Greenhead (3) and Fell Side (4–5). In centuries past they were inextricably linked to the vibrant mining ventures whose now-sealed galleries pepper the Caldbeck Fells.

Ascent from Longlands 26

Via the upper Ellen valley →4km/2½ miles ↑445m/1460ft ⏱2hr

The natural line along the beck leaves the ascent to the end.

1 Go through the gate and at once bear right off the main green track, ford the beck and follow on, taking a track that leads south, close beside a wall, above Longlands Beck. Pass below the spoil of a gated mine-level, and after a ruined shed pursue the green track under **Lowthwaite Fell**. As the marshes of the infant **River Ellen** are neared bend left (east), with no clear path until you reach a sheep trod running along the base of the bracken slope. At a confluence, ford the river and follow the tongue up by a ruined fold to reach the head of the slope. Here take a

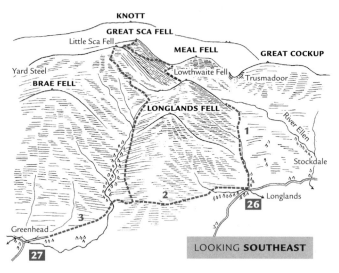

LOOKING **SOUTHEAST**

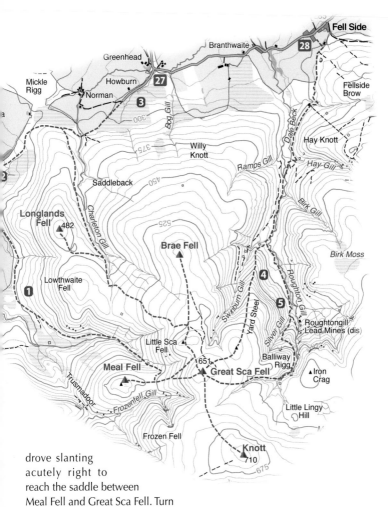

drove slanting
acutely right to
reach the saddle between
Meal Fell and Great Sca Fell. Turn
left to follow the ridge path. There are two options: one path goes directly up
the fell to the top, while another forks left, slanting at an easier angle up to
the depression between Little and Great Sca Fells, where you turn right to the
summit.

Ascent from Longlands 26 or Greenhead 27

Via Charleton Gill →4.6km/3 miles ↑440m/1445ft ⏱2hr 10min

A steady gradient all the way to the top, equally logical from Longlands or Greenhead

Cairn and wind-break on Little Sca Fell

2 From Longlands follow the green track leading off from the gate and curving from north-east to east over the ridge-end of **Longlands Fell**. As you pass a shallow pit reach a low wooden sign guiding right for 'Great Sca Fell'. This consistent bridle path leads up the **Charleton Gill** valley. The track runs on out of the valley and climbs the long slope linking Lowthwaite Fell with Little Sca Fell. Coming onto the ridge path from Brae Fell, switch up right, taking in the summit of **Little Sca Fell** if you wish. The continuing ridge path heads on southeast to dip and then rise to the main summit.

3 From Greenhead follow the open road leading southwest, passing **Howburn**. At a fork in the way the road becomes a track, signed 'Public Way, Longlands and Cumbria Way': follow this to ford **Charleton Gill** and turn left (south) to join Route **2** to the summit.

Ascent from Fell Side 28

Make a beeline up the northeastern spur or follow the gill for a more roundabout route with a little more variety.

Via Yard Steel →4.1km/2½ miles ↑405m/1330ft ⏱1hr 45min

4 Pass up through the fell gate and follow the open track right to enter the main Dale Beck valley. Pass above the foundations of the mine smelt mill to come by a sheepfold beside the **Hay Gill** footbridge. Cross the bridge.

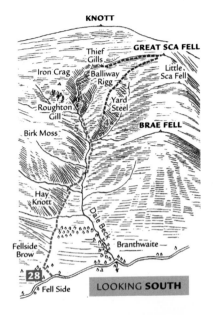

KNOTT

GREAT SCA FELL

Thief
Gills

Iron Crag
Balliway
Rigg

Little
Sca Fell

Roughton
Gill

Yard
Steel

BRAE FELL

Birk Moss

Hay
Knott

Dale Beck

Fellside
Brow

Branthwaite

28

Fell Side

LOOKING **SOUTH**

Stride on and cross the next footbridge spanning Dale Beck. Continue on along the old mine access track, on the west side of the dale bottom, with the steep grass slopes of Brae Fell and Yard Steel looming to the right. Cross the ford of Swinburn Gill and step up onto the ridge through the brief mantle of bracken, glancing back down on the elongated sheepfold. Set to work climbing Yard Steel. The fine grass of its early stages is replaced by tougher stuff higher up, where a right-hand bias will prove easier on the ankles. Pass by the cairn, a cluster of stones gathered

Dale Beck valley towards Yard Steel

from elsewhere, marking the top of the gently domed prairie. A path leads on briefly south-southwest towards the main summit, although this tends to be lost upon crossing the old shepherds' drove. Proceed to reach the cairned top.

Via Balliway Rigg →5.1km/3¼ miles ↑410m/1345ft ⊕2hr 15min

5 Set off with Route **4** but stick with the dale-bottom track, coming by the low remnant walls of mine buildings to embark on the grass trod winding up the ridge ahead. Starting on the west side, overlooking **Silver Gill**, cross two lateral paths before switching left to come over the brow above the dramatic **Roughton Gill** ravine. The grass trod contours over looser slopes as it moves into the upper ravine.

Ford the beck and arrive at the confluence with **Thief Gills**, where any hint of a path disappears, although a trace can be sensed to the left, leading south past a sheepfold. Bear up the right-hand ravine, with volcanic nodules outcropping, and come up the bank to climb onto the moorland ridge of **Balliway Rigg**. Head on west, with nothing more than the odd sheep track to ease progress on the rough peaty ridge to the summit.

Waterfall in Roughton Gill

The summit

Resting on the broad, rough, grassy domed summit, the metre-high cairn is a meeting point of three paths. Like that of its higher neighbour Knott, the fell's cairn is not a place walkers will wish to idle long. (The better station is the cairn on Little Sca Fell.)

Safe descents

Essentially, keep to the grassy ridges – for Fell Side NE then N down Yard Steel (**4**), passing its cairn, and for Longlands N over Little Sca Fell (**2**) and via the bridle path down the Charleton Gill valley.

Ridge routes

Brae Fell → *1.6km/1 mile* ↓*85m/280ft* ↑*15m/50ft* ⏲*30min*
Head NW to the cairn and low shelter on Little Sca Fell and continue on down the bank to run on with minimal gradient N to the large cairn.

Knott → *1km/½ mile* ↓*15m/50ft* ↑*70m/235ft* ⏲*20min*
A strong ridge path curves from S to SE up to the plateau-top cairn.

Longlands Fell → *2.5km/1½ mile* ↓*230m/755ft* ↑*55m/180ft* ⏲*40min*
Head NW to the cairn and wind-break on Little Sca Fell. Swing down the bank, now with a prominent path leading generally W down to Broad Moss, then keep initially to the obvious quad track descending NNW above Charleton Gill before aiming W into the damp saddle and rising NW by a hoary old cairn to the summit.

Meal Fell → *0.9km/½ mile* ↓*130m/430ft* ↑*25m/80ft* ⏲*20min*
Head W down the steep west slope to the wide depression (or head NW to the saddle and then SW across the slope to the same point) and continue on W to rise up the east slope to the summit.

16 HIGH PIKE 658M/2159FT

Climb it from	Fell Side 28, Nether Row 29, Hesket Newmarket 30, Carrock Beck 31 or Grainsgill Bridge 34
Character	Caldbeck's backyard fell with grand perspectives towards Scotland from the northern flank
Fell-friendly route	9
Summit grid ref	NY 318 350
Link it with	Carrock Fell or Knott
Part of	The Northern Crown

The beginning or the end of the Lake District – whatever your perspective, High Pike holds a unique position, recognised by the Cumbria Way, which makes a point of tracking over its top on its long march between Carlisle and Ulverston. The fell's unassuming grassy slopes belie an amazingly diverse mineral content and you may spot crystalline fragments of rock sparkling in the sun. And with no less than three mines – Potts Gill, Sandbed and Driggeth – held within the becks and gills that have their origin here, it was also clearly pivotal in the extraction industry hereabouts.

↑ *High Pike from the slopes of Miton Hill*

Sooner or later most ascents come upon the surface scars of mining. Rake hollows, spoil, fenced cavities and various low-walled structures betray the industrious subterranean workings for mineral wealth that took place in past decades. All is quiet today, although natural regrowth on the poisoned earth banks is scant.

With road access from three sides, it is no wonder that the fell is well endowed with possible routes of ascent. The principal routes begin from the north and east at Fell Side (1–3), Nether Row (4), Calebreck and Carrock Beck (7–9), and, more distantly, from Hesket Newmarket (5–6). Two routes rise from southerly Mosedale (10–11).

Ascent from Fell Side 28

Via Fellside Brow → *3.2km/2 miles* ↑*370m/1210ft* ⏱*1hr 20min*

1 Pass up through the gate and follow the open track right, then after 100 metres break left, guided by a blue bridleway waymark post. This puts the walk onto a rising green track which climbs easily up **Fellside Brow**. A second waymark post guides left at a fork. Now on easier grass terrain, bend right at the next fork and come over a lateral mine track, crossing a flattened area of

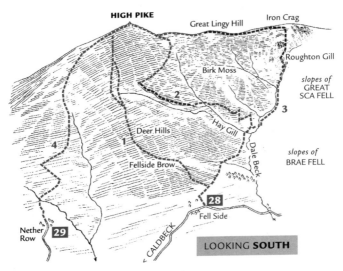

spoil, with a small bield adjacent. Rise up the next bank and come between fenced rakes, with a larger H-shaped bield above. The trail comes onto the plateau of **Deer Hills**. There are two regular ways from here, one climbing the slope ahead to High Pike's northern shelter and another taking the grass track sweeping round the western flank and then approaching the summit from the south side.

Above Hay Gill → *5.4km/3½ miles* ↑*455m/1495ft* ⌚*2hr*

A wanderers' way by quiet sheep walks

2 Start out with Route **1** but then keep with the green track as it leads into the Dale Beck valley. After crossing the **Hay Gill** footbridge come round the bank and ascend left, quickly coming through the bracken onto a groove path slanting right. This green trod follows two exaggerated hairpins to rise steadily up the breast of the fell. Higher up, the trod is lost in the rough moor grass. (Do not be tempted just to drift up **Birk Hill**.) Bear left and then find the shallow grooves that betray the old drove, which leads down to a more obvious track near the gill confluence. Ford the southern gill and then step up the tongue, without the aid of a path, rising on the moor grass to cross a lateral drove and reach an **old adit**. Turn right along the next drove. This leads south and curves up onto the ridge to join the skyline ridge path and climb north to the summit.

Via Roughton Gill → *6.6km/4 miles* ↑*465m/1530ft* ⌚*2hr 20min*

Revel in the intricate charms of Roughton Gill and bonus ridge-walking by sneaking up from the south.

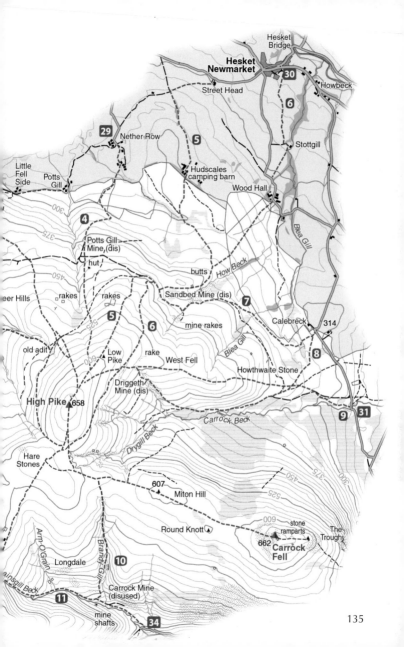

Hesket
Bridge
**Hesket
Newmarket**
Howbeck
30
Street Head
6
Stottgill
29 Nether Row
5
Little
Fell
Side
Potts
Gill
Hudscales
camping barn
Wood Hall
Blea Gill
4
Potts Gill
Mine (dis)
hut
butts
How Beck
eer Hills
rakes
rakes
Sandbed Mine (dis)
7
mine rakes
Calebreck
5
6
314
old adit
Low
Pike
rake
West Fell
Blea Gill
8
Driggeth
Mine (dis)
Howthwaite Stone
High Pike ▲658
Carrock Beck
9 **31**
Hare
Stones
Drygill Beck
607
Miton Hill
Arm O'Grain
Branda Gill
Round Knott ⊙
stone
ramparts
662 **Carrock
Fell**
The
Trough
Longdale
10
ainsgill Beck
Carrock Mine
(disused)
11
mine
shafts
34

135

Mosedale from the Lingy Hut

3 Follow Route **2** to the point where it starts to zig-zag steeply up the bracken hillside. Here continue along the beckside path to cross the **Dale Beck** foot-bridge and follow the track on the west side of the dale floor. When you reach the dale head, ford the beck and pass the pump-house to work up into the ravine beside **Roughton Gill**. The ground is unstable but not difficult – it's more stumbling than scrambling. Follow the natural inclination and progress up onto the **Iron Crag** felltop, where there is a cairn. From here head east-southeast, avoiding the marsh of **Miller Moss** and passing old shooting butts en route to the **Lingy Hut**. Turn left and keep on with the ridge path to the summit.

Ascent from Nether Row 29

A direct line in the footsteps of the miners

Via Potts Gill Mine →*3.2km/2 miles* ↑*395m/1295ft* ⏱*1hr 20min*
4 Follow the bridle-lane signed 'Potts Gill' through the charming environs of Clay Bottom Farm. Gates lead to an open track which duly swings left then hairpins right, climbing to pass beneath a spoil bank. When the track forks, keep to the left-hand rising green track which runs on over a lateral track.

Soon spot a tiny **hut** in a nook to the left. The green-way rises, passing close to the right of a collapsed mineral rake, with a mine air-shaft over to the right. The route heads up the fellside, now as a simple fell trod, onto the plain ridge-top to reach the northern shelter. Continue on to the summit.

Ascent from Hesket Newmarket 30

Combine these two routes for an excellent figure-of-eight expedition through the site of Sandbed Mine.

Via Hudscales and Low Pike →*5.2km/3¼ miles* ↑*495m/1620ft* ⏲*2hr 25min*
5 Take the westward by-road from the head of the village street to **Street Head** and follow the lovely footpath signed 'Nether Row' through the back-lawn passage and then predominantly in a lane. Part-way along encounter the Hudscales Farm road. Turn left and follow this up to and through the farm-yard, guided by the camping-barn sign. A gate in the shelter-belt wall gives access to the open moor. Follow the quad track south to join a footpath. This bends half-right to join a green track leading up from Wood Hall, by grouse butts and past the spoil and waste of the old **Sandbed Mine**. Turn right onto

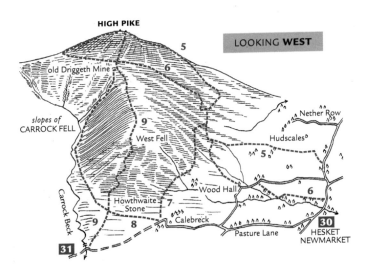

Summit, featuring a memorial bench for contemplating the far-off Galloway Hills

the old lateral mine track, bear left, then take the second track rising left to step off this onto a walkers' path which climbs the northern slope unhindered to the cairn on **Low Pike**. Persist beyond on a thin path, passing the shelter to reach the summit.

Via Wood Hall →6.8km/4¼ miles ↑490m/1615ft ⏱2hr 45min

6 Follow the footpath heading south from the car park. This popular path leads by a string of eight fields, with stiles and gates, and crosses the access lane to **Stottgill** to reach the minor road. Turn left and pass through the environs of **Wood Hall**. At the left-hand bend go through the gate and cross the dam. Walk up through a galvanised gate in a lateral fence to climb the pasture to a ladder-stile at the top. Here join the turf path which leads up to the old **Sandbed Mine** site. Joining the mine track at this point, go right and take the first track, which hairpins left to rise steadily up the fellside and come above the **Driggeth Mine**. Watch for the path that steps up right, slanting to the summit.

Ascent from Carrock Beck 31

Routes 7 and 8 could instead be tackled from the car park at Calebreck, less than a kilometre's walk up the road to the north.

Via Sandbed Mine →4km/2½ miles ↑350m/1150ft ⏱1hr 45min

Combine this route with Route 8 or 9 in descent for a pleasing circuit.

7 From the common, start by walking a short kilometre up the road to the car park just short of **Calebreck**. Follow the green track leading off in a westward direction. This curves up above the intake wall and comes to the environs of the old **Sandbed Mine**. Here join either Route **5** or **6** to reach the summit.

Via Driggeth Mine →3.6km/2¼ miles ↑355m/1165ft ⏱1hr 20min

8 As with Route **7**, from the common walk up the road to **Calebreck**. An open bridle-track leads west from the roadside, and a matter of paces from the car park a low sign directs left onto a grass path. This lovely turf trail sweeps easily across the open pasture, passing some 100 metres from the **Howthwaite Stone**. It converges with a more obvious track as it comes into the **Carrock Beck** valley. Follow this upstream to begin a steady climb above a ravine and pass the spoil banks of the old **Driggeth Mine**. Coming onto a lateral mine road bear left and almost at once step onto a path which slants up the felltop pasture to the shelter and on to the summit.

Via West Fell →3.5km/2¼ miles ↑395m/1300ft ⏱1hr 45min

A lovely direct climb

9 Cross the footbridge and bear left almost immediately off the rising roadway. Coming over a track follow the quad track through and above the bracken, crossing a further lateral track and heading up the grassy fell-slope ahead. A definite path winds up onto the **West Fell** ridge. Keep a southerly bias as you follow this onto the track that comes above the site of the old **Driggeth Mine** to meet the lateral track. Go left with the track along the eastern slope to meet the ridge path, and here switch back north to the summit cairn.

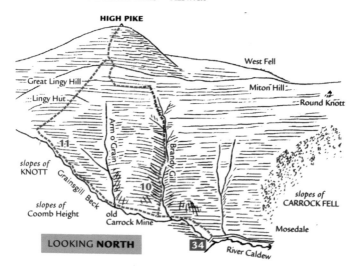

HIGH PIKE

West Fell

Great Lingy Hill

Miton Hill

Lingy Hut

Round Knott

Arm o' Grain

Brandy Gill

11

slopes of
KNOTT

Grainsgill Beck

10

slopes of
CARROCK FELL

slopes of
Coomb Height

old
Carrock Mine

Mosedale

LOOKING **NORTH**

34

River Caldew

Ascent from Grainsgill Bridge 34

*Another opportunity for an excellent loop following the line of the waterways
up to the ridges to the south*

Via Brandy Gill →3km/2 miles ↑355m/1165ft ⏱1hr 30min

10 Step up from the bridge on the green-way or, more logically, from the
barrier along the old
tarmac mine road.
Follow this roadway
northwest. The route
turns acutely right on
an old green track.
This slices through
the lower portion of
the western extrac-
tion gully, rises and
then breaks off to
follow the feature up

Brandy Gill and a mine level

the heather bank towards the fence that (rather weakly) shields the first deep shaft, overlain with rusty pipes. Keep to the right, rising to a second fenced shaft, equally exposed – **take care**. A continuing path, of little more than sheep-trod proportions, leads on to pass over a loose gully, with prominent quartz visible. Keep largely within the ravine. Be aware that the small fenced shaft up the slope is **every bit as dangerous** as the previous ones.

Contour to pass a sheepfold and pass above the next mare's-tail waterfall. Traces of a path lead to a third waterfall, with a short adit. Keep to the ravine until, after areas of boulder scree, a grassy amphitheatre opens. Take the right-hand grassy hollow leading up onto the moor. Pass the fenced area and cross a grassy expanse to join the ridge path. Turn left following the main way, which curves round the head of Drygill Beck to cross a mine track as it rises north to the summit.

Via Grainsgill Beck →4km/2½ miles ↑375m/1230ft ☺1hr 30min

The Lingy Hut bothy beside the Cumbria Way

11 Short of Grainsgill Bridge follow the old mine road (still tarmacked in its initial stages and part of the high-level section of the Cumbria Way) with Route 10. It leads on beyond the few traces of Carrock Mine. The track becomes a path as it progresses upstream, fording Arm o'Grain, and meets the more regular ridge connection at the edge of Miller Moss. Here turn right, passing the Lingy Hut and continuing with Route 3 to complete the climb.

The summit

Being the northernmost fell in the national park grants High Pike the distinction of a wide northward view. Most eyes will be trained on the far horizon and the hills of Scotland beyond the Solway and Carlisle, although some will also allow their gaze to drift east to the North Pennines – a romantic outlook.

Safe descents

Stick to tried and tested trails to be sure of avoiding the mine shafts. For Fell Side a path leads NNW (**1**), for Nether Row head NE then N (**4**), for Hesket Newmarket go NE to join the mine track that runs along the high shelf on the east of the fell (**6**) and for Calebreck cross this track to go by West Fell (**9**).

Ridge routes

Carrock Fell →*3.2km/2 miles* ↓*100m/330ft* ↑*100m/330ft* ☺*1hr*
Walk S to cross the lateral track and skirt the head of Drygill Beck by curving E. The ridge path dips at the head of Red Gate and rises to the cairned summit of Miton Hill. Walk past the rocks and reach an unavoidable peaty morass, with the path in doubt, until firm ground reappears on the stony rise to the summit of Carrock.

Knott →*3.6km/2¼ miles* ↓*115m/375ft* ↑*170m/560ft* ☺*1hr 10min*
Walk S to join the prominent track on leveller ground. This leads SW to come over Great Lingy Hill and pass the Lingy Hut. After fording the upper course of Grainsgill Beck at the edge of Miller Moss, the route swings W on the rise onto Knott's broad east ridge, the path an unfailing guide to the summit cairn.

Carrock Fell from the head of Drygill Beck

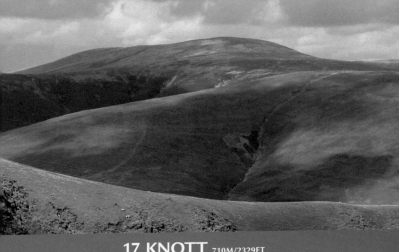

17 KNOTT 710M/2329FT

Climb it from	Horsemoor Hills **22**, Longlands **26**, Fell Side **28** or Grainsgill Bridge **34**
Character	A high, shy fell at the heart of the Northern Fells
Fell-friendly route	2
Summit grid ref	NY 296 329
Link it with	Great Calva, Great Sca Fell or High Pike
Part of	The Northern Crown

Quite the hub and focus of the Back o' Skidda group, Knott invariably features as a high turning-point in a circuit of its satellite summits. Lacking distinctive form, its greatest virtue is its gentle paternal presence, particularly above Hause Gill to the west and the silver ribbon of the juvenile Caldew to the east. Adding a little extra charm, in season those eastern ridges are clothed in a mantle of purple heather, fit to rival neighbouring Great Calva.

Grouse live contented lives these days, as excited guns no longer spring menacingly from the deserted grouse butts. Note the curiously descriptive, monosyllabic names hereabouts – 'Coomb', 'Knott', 'Pike', 'Rigg' and 'Snab' – which suggest late coinage, perhaps associated with the golden age of grouse shooting.

As befits the fell's presidential status, routes lead up from ridges and valleys in all directions, with longer expeditions from the north and west (1–3) and shorter, sharper ascents from the east (4–7).

↑ *Knott over Tarn Crags, from above Bowscale Tarn* 143

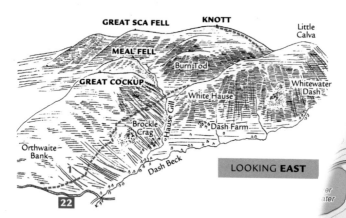

LOOKING **EAST**

Ascent from Horsemoor Hills 22

Via Hause Gill →5.4km/3½ miles ↑540m/1770ft ⏰2hr 10min

A lovely level route, leaving the ascent to the end

1 Walk north to the farm track which leaves the minor road between Orthwaite and Horsemoor Hills. Follow the bridle-lane leading south, signed 'Burn Tod 3 miles', to the low farm track. Turn off 100 metres after the second quarry with the bridleway signposted 'Burn Tod', a lovely turf trail ascending southeast. This comes over the broad shoulder above **Brockle Crag** and heads on as a comparatively level track along the southern slopes of **Great Cockup**, then duly drifts downward to ford **Burntod Gill**. Cross marshy patches on your way up the **Hause Gill** valley, getting close to the gill in its upper ravine and emerging onto the ridge at the grassy saddle. Join the ridge path, turn left and follow the initially steep, grassy path direct to the summit.

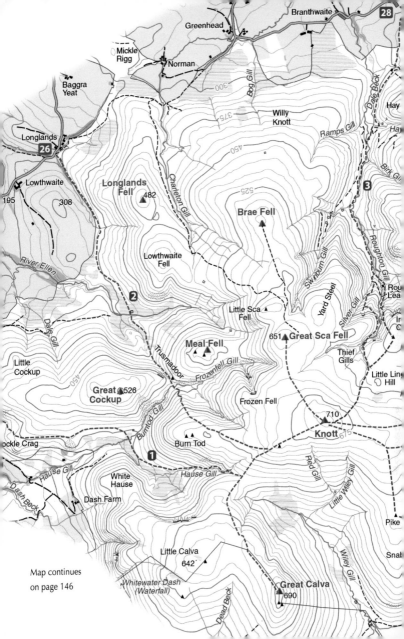

Map continues
on page 146

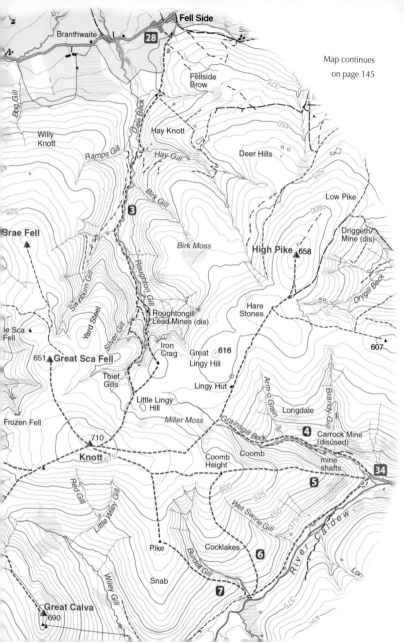

Map continues
on page 145

Fell Side

Branthwaite

28

Fellside
Brow

Hay Knott

Willy
Knott

Bog Gill

Ramps Gill

Dale Beck

Hay Gill

Birk Gill

Deer Hills

375

450

525

3

Birk Moss

High Pike ▲658

Low Pike

Driggeth
Mine (dis)

600

525

Brae Fell ▲

Swinburn Gill

Roughton Gill

Yard Steel

Silver Gill

Roughtongill
Lead Mines (dis)

Hare
Stones

Drygill Beck

le Sca
Fell ▲

607

651 ▲ Great Sca Fell

Iron
Crag

Great
Lingy Hill

616

Thief
Gills

Little Lingy
Hill

Lingy Hut

Arm o' Grain

Longdale

Brandy Gill

Frozen Fell

710

Miller Moss

Grainsgill Beck

4 Carrock Mine
(disused)

Knott

676

Coomb

mine
shafts

34

Red Gill

Little Wiley Gill

Coomb
Height

5

600

525

450

375

Wet Swine Gill

River Caldew

Pike

Cocklakes

6

Snab

Burdell Gill

7

Wiley Gill

Great Calva
▲690

450

375

Lon

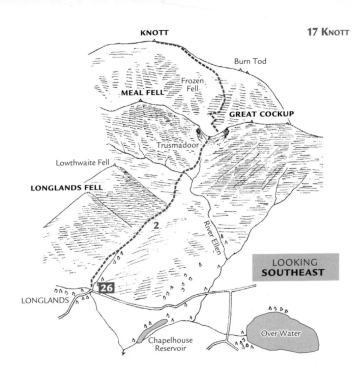

Burn Tod

Frozen
Fell

MEAL FELL

GREAT COCKUP

Trusmadoor

Lowthwaite Fell

LONGLANDS FELL

2

River Ellen

LOOKING
SOUTHEAST

26

LONGLANDS

Chapelhouse
Reservoir

Over Water

Ascent from Longlands 26

Via Trusmadoor →*5.1km/3¼ miles* ↑*525m/1725ft* ⏱*2hr 15min*

Head directly to and through Trusmadoor, on good paths almost all the way.

2 Go through the gate and at once bear right off the green track, ford the beck and follow a track which leads south, close beside a wall, above Longlands Beck. Pass below the spoil of a gated mine-level, and after a ruined shed pursue the green track to ford the infant **River Ellen**. The path leads up beside the esker (glacial ridge) to thread through the **Trusmadoor** pass. Ford **Burntod Gill** and follow the succeeding path as it winds up the fellside of **Burn Tod**, passing peat groughs as it drifts east. The trace of a path is quickly lost in the rough moor terrain. Forge on east to come onto the grassy ridge path as it eases up onto the summit.

Ascent from Fell Side 28

Via Roughton Gill →5.2km/3¼ miles ↑485m/1590ft ⊕2hr

A most enjoyable approach, with a variant over Balliway Rigg, the tough final tramp above Thief Gills easily forgiven

3 Follow the regular track, an old road to the mines at the head of Dale Beck, and see the tumbling foundations of a smelt mill under Hay Knott on the way into the Dale Beck valley. The track crosses two footbridges spanning Hay Gill and Dale Beck as it wanders purposefully up-dale. After passing the ruins of old lead-mine buildings ford Roughton Gill. Walk to the left of the pump-house and clamber up the scarred slope, keeping close to the ravine. The earthy slope makes for unsteady progress. From the higher fall follow the sheep path left, breaking away from the ravine onto the fellside, and climb without the aid of a path to the high rim to find a sheep trod along the edge. Leave this to quickly reach the substantial cairn on the moorland top of Iron Crag. From here head south-southwest over the featureless plateau of Little Lingy Hill to climb entirely pathless to the summit.

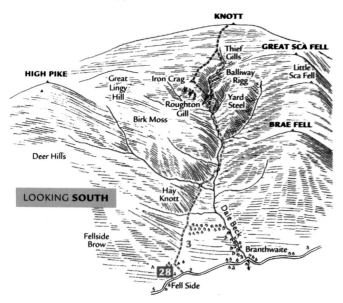

Looking down Thief Gills

Alternatively, instead of fording Roughton Gill, bear up onto the grass trod winding up the prominent tongue of **Balliway Rigg** ahead. Initially on its west side, overlooking Silver Gill, cross two lateral paths before switching left to come over the brow above the exciting Roughton Gill ravine. The grass trod contours over looser slopes as it moves into the upper ravine. After fording the beck, soon reach the confluence with **Thief Gills**. Ford this and keep south, passing a sheepfold, to trudge pathlessly over **Little Lingy Hill** southwest to the summit.

Ascent from Grainsgill Bridge 34

Pair low-level, intricate Route 4 with ridge-walking Route 5 for a lovely east–west loop.

Via Grainsgill Beck →*3.4km/2 miles* ↑*410m/1345ft* ⏰*1hr 45min*
4 Short of Grainsgill Bridge follow the old mine road (still tarmacked in its initial stages and part of the high-level section of the Cumbria Way). The road leads on beyond the few traces of the once-considerable **Carrock Mine**, becoming a path as it progresses upstream. Ford **Arm o'Grain** and continue up to meet the ridge connection at the edge of **Miller Moss**. Bear left then

149

keep to the right-hand path and mount the facing blunt ridge southwest onto the moor of **Rigg**. Head west from here to the summit.

Via Coomb Height →*3.2km/2 miles* ↑*410m/1345ft* ⏱*1hr 45min*
5 Just beyond Grainsgill Bridge take a clear path stepping up through the bracken on the south side, climbing into the heather and over an old mining-rake trench (dangerously exposed at one point). Despite the heather the going is agreeable. Stick resolutely to the ridge to climb on a thin trod to the solitary cairn on **Coomb Height**. The hard work is over, although it still seems a long way to the summit (1.5km). A choice of two tracks leads west. Take the more southerly line over a largely grassy moor to the summit.

Via Cocklakes →*4.8km/3 miles* ↑*425m/1390ft* ⏱*2hr 15min*

An old shooters' track

6 Follow the open track on from Grainsgill Bridge (signed to Skiddaw House) for about 2km. Having crossed **Wet Swine Gill**, on the approach to the ford of **Burdell Gill** find a green-way switching acutely right. Follow this unerringly up the open heather flanks of **Cocklakes**. The consistent path sadly dissolves on reaching the plateau. Cross the moor to the cairn on **Coomb Height**, then turn left to follow Route **5** along the narrow ridge track to the summit.

Looking to Carrock Fell from the cairn on Coomb Height

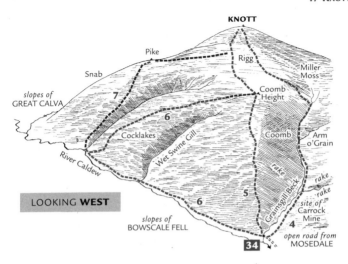

KNOTT

Pike

Rigg

Snab

Miller Moss

slopes of
GREAT CALVA

Coomb Height

7

6

Cocklakes

Coomb

Arm o'Grain

Wet Swine Gill

River Caldew

rake

LOOKING **WEST**

5

Grainsgill Beck

rake

rake

6

site of Carrock Mine

slopes of
BOWSCALE FELL

4

34

open road from
MOSEDALE

Via Pike →*4.6km/3 miles* ↑*420m/1380ft* ⏱*2hr 10min*

Little-frequented and largely pathless up Snab's remote ridge

7 Keep company with Route **6** as far as **Burdell Gill**. Here ford the gill and bear right up the bank above the birches. The initial sheep path is quickly lost, consumed by dense heather on the site of a former series of grouse butts. The heather duly relents, and a seasonal faint quad track comes underfoot. Cresting the **Snab** ridge reach the cairn on **Pike**. Sheep trods lead on north along the flat ridge and up the flank of **Rigg**, at the top of which your way is left (west), joining Route **6** to the summit.

The summit

The summit cairn stands in proud isolation at the centre of an expansive summit plateau, and as a result the view is limited. The best places to sit for refreshment lie along the southern edge, from where a lovely view opens up through the Glenderaterra gap into the heart of the Lakeland fells, with the Scafells and Great Gable peering over the top of Lonscale Fell.

Safe descents

In mist keep to well-evidenced paths, although that leading E to Coomb Height (**5**) for Mosedale is less clear than you might hope. The ridge path leading SW then W via Hause Gill (**1**) makes a useful route, while points north are best reached via the summit of Great Sca Fell.

Ridge routes

Great Calva →2.6km/1½ miles ↓160m/525ft ↑135m/445ft ⏱45min
Follow the path leading SW from the summit cairn. After a small cairn the path plummets to a minor saddle at the head of Hause Gill. As the continuing path rises watch for the fork before the pools then take the left-hand path, which leads up to a stile in the ridge fence. Cross this and follow on SE to the summit.

Great Sca Fell → 1km/½ mile
↓70m/235ft ↑15m/50ft ⏱25min
A strong ridge path curves from NW to N down to the cairn on the grassy domed summit.

High Pike →3.6km/2¼ miles
↓170m/560ft ↑115m/375ft ⏱1hr 10min
Head due E on an apparent path which then dips off the plateau NE to the head of Grainsgill Beck, below the marshy hollow of Miller Moss. Pass the Lingy Hut on a clear track which rises easily over Hare Stones. Where a S–N path crosses, step off the main contouring track and walk up N to the summit cairn.

Summit cairn in winter

18 LATRIGG 368M/1207FT

Climb it from	Keswick or Gale Road 5
Character	Bringing (wheelchair-accessible) joy to visitors great and small with its panoramic views over Keswick and Derwentwater
Fell-friendly route	7
Summit grid ref	NY 279 247

With its wonderful situation – in the lap of Skiddaw and perfectly poised above Keswick – Latrigg is a gentle fell for all the family. Its slopes clothed in trees and its summit acres carpeted with verdant pasture, in good weather this lowly belvedere is transformed into a viewpoint par excellence: a scenic extravaganza of mountains, lakes, crags and woods, near and far. Anyone newly arrived in the area – whatever their fellwalking credentials – would be wise to make this modest top a first objective.

At its base the Railway Footpath adds further opportunities to explore the gorge of the River Greta, especially in combination with Brundholme Wood. Join it from the town (beside the leisure centre, site of the old station) or wend your way from Threlkeld (once the restoration work in the wake of the 2015 floods is complete) or stroll down from the eastern tip of Latrigg's access land.

↑ *Latrigg from Crow Park in Keswick*

Such a popular fell naturally has many routes – from the graded and clearly signposted to the steep and, frankly, obscure. All can be reached direct from Keswick town centre but parking on Gale Road minimises the ascent and maximises the accessibility.

Ascent from Keswick

The town's favourite fell is a short stroll from the town centre.

Follow Brundholme Road left (northwest) from the mini roundabout just behind the leisure centre to a road-fork.

Via Spooney Green Lane and Mallen Dodd →3.2km/2 miles ↑295m/965ft ⏱1hr 30min

1 Keep left at the road-fork to reach the start of **Spooney Green Lane** (on the right) and stride up the lane. Cross the hubbub of the **A66** to a hand-gate at Spooney Green. Keep with the rising track by two further hand-gates, coming above **Ewe How** and arriving at an information panel. For the most comfortable ascent, continue until the formal way is signed right to 'Latrigg summit'. This path makes exaggerated zig-zags up the bracken-clad fellside and climbs at an easy angle onto the shoulder of **Mallen Dodd**. Come to a gill-head

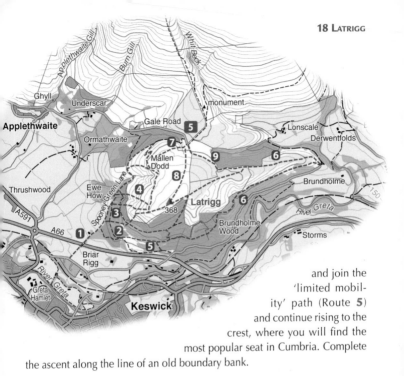

and join the 'limited mobility' path (Route **5**) and continue rising to the crest, where you will find the most popular seat in Cumbria. Complete the ascent along the line of an old boundary bank.

The most popular seat in Cumbria?

Via the western scarp →*1.8km/1¼ miles* ↑*275m/895ft* ⊙*1hr*

Three routes clamber off Spooney Green Lane through the thorns, broadleaves and conifers onto the steep bracken slope – with little to recommend them in ascent and even less in descent.

2 Start out on Spooney Green Lane with Route **1** but step up off the track the moment the meadow view first opens, after the last 'Hens in lane' notice and the gate on the right where the Brundholme woodland walk begins. The impromptu path clambers up to cross a lateral bridle-track then heads more steeply up the slope, with dense conifers close right, to cross a second track on Whinny Brow. Quickly rise to a fixed hand-gate and broken fence accessing the open fell. Climb steeply onto a shoulder of the west ridge to complete the ascent.

3 Alternatively, continue up Spooney Green Lane until it converges with a track from a gate acute right. Turn right, go through the adjacent hand-gate and, a matter of a few paces further on, step up the bank and ascend through the broadleaved woodland to the upper track. Only now do you enter the conifers up a very steep passage which is most unpleasant and slippery when wet. Cross the stile and forge your way to the skyline and the summit.

4 The best of a bad bunch continues up Spooney Green Lane beyond a gill crossing and, where the path encounters gorse and sweeps right as two separate paths, turns up right at the cross-ways into the woodland. This path quickly forks. Keep up left, rising to a stile. Climb up the bracken-free path strip from here to reach the summit.

Via Brundholme Wood →*1.2km/¾ mile* ↑*215m/705ft* ⊙*50min*

A direct woodland approach from the old road to Westcoe

5 Turn right at the road-fork beyond the roundabout north of the leisure centre to pass the entrance to Greta Bank Veterinary Centre and carry on by Windebrowe (part of the Calvert Trust) to cross the A66 Keswick bypass. Having crossed the A66 step left to begin a direct climb almost entirely 'lost' in the mantle of trees immediately south of the summit. Bear left then up right to a gate and a path-junction. Turn back right on the path merging acutely

from the right, which leads through gorse to arrive at the point where the more direct path crosses (and Route **6** continues on).

Here turn sharp left to climb the flight of steps to a hairpin and continue up the woodland bank. The path comes through more gorse and climbs on, partly in conifers, to arrive at a lateral forest track. Go right, and after 140 metres step up and enter a coniferous tunnel. This leads through the gloom to a fence-stile. Emerge into daylight and complete the ascent beside the boundary bank/wall. At the top, beside a gate, go left and very shortly reach the summit.

Via the east ridge →*3.2km/2 miles* ↑*215m/705ft* ⏱*1hr 20min*

Extend your outing a little to savour those southward views.

6 Set out with Route **5**, but from the gate and path junction keep with the east-bearing path, contouring through the wood for a kilometre. Emerge from the trees and continue on to traverse the lower slopes of Latrigg's east ridge towards Brundholme. Reach a gate at the side of the road and turn sharply back left, following a sign to 'Latrigg summit'. (It's possible to reach this point from the Keswick Railway Footpath by following the roadway that winds up past the dwelling at Brundholme.) The rutted track soon becomes an open green track which gently gains height. At the next gate join a path bending half-left. This rises to cross and accompany an old boundary bank, then drifts slightly left to keep along the edge of the scarp, climbing up through a gate to the summit.

157

A sign points the way to the summit from Gale Road, backed by Skiddaw Little Man

Ascent from Gale Road 5

Via the 'limited mobility' path →*1.4km/1 mile* ↑*90m/300ft* ⏲*40min*

A joyous path which deserves its regular flow of happy strollers

7 A simple, carefully graded path leads from the footpath sign at the Gale Road lane-end gate, keeping to the rise of the western escarpment. The views are consistently uplifting. Follow on assuredly to the summit.

Direct →*0.6km/½ mile* ↑*65m/215ft* ⏲*25min*
8 From the lane-end gate leave the obvious path and head due south, striding up the gently sloping pasture amid contented sheep to reach the summit unhindered.

Via the east ridge →*2.3km/1½ miles* ↑*230m/760ft* ⊕*1hr*

Linger a little on the quieter northeastern slopes.

9 Follow the open track leading southeast from the lane-end gate. Beyond a gate at the woodland corner follow on until a path is spotted converging acutely from the right, short of the next gate. Turn right onto this open-pasture path, rising over the line of an old boundary bank, and follow this up with a low escarpment close left. The path rises to a gate and duly comes above woodland to arrive at the unmarked summit.

The summit

The summit is proof, if proof were needed, that height is not everything when it comes to generous viewpoints. While fellwalkers extol the merits of Skiddaw Little Man for its 'high in the sky' prospect down into the heart of the Lakeland fells, Latrigg is more intimate and accessible to anyone who wishes to wander to its scarp edge.

Safe descents

While all of the routes described are practical in descent, the best choice would be N and then SW (**1**) for Keswick or just NE (**8**) for Gale Road.

19 LING FELL 373M/1224FT

Climb it from	Brumston Bridge **12** or Embleton Church **11**
Character	A lesser-known summit of the northwestern corner, graced with broad green trails sweeping up to wide Solway views
Fell-friendly route	1
Summit grid ref	NY 179 286

A little distant from a main road, and without any striking features to catch the eye, outlying Ling Fell is overlooked by many a visiting walker, but those who live hereabouts value its simple charms. On a sunny Sunday afternoon this is the perfect not-so-gentle leg-stretch, with lovely views to boot. As the name suggests, its slopes are shrouded in heather – a purple blaze in late summer.

In times past, as the heather started to bloom local sportsmen would have gathered to disturb the stock of grouse. Only the tumbled shooting butts remain today. Another historic feature on the northern slopes, the Corpse Road, must once have linked the little church in Chapel Wood to the east with the consecrated ground at St Cuthbert's, Embleton.

This little mound can be quickly climbed (1–2) or girdled at a more leisurely pace in an almost-perfect circle (3).

↑ *Ling Fell from the fell path west of Kelswick Farm*

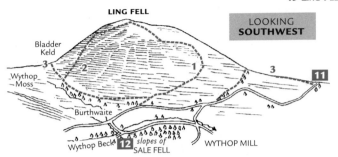

Ascent from Brumston Bridge 12

Via the northern slopes →2.4km/1½ miles ↑330m/1080ft ⏱1hr

Follow the old Corpse Road to survey the secluded Wythop valley from above.

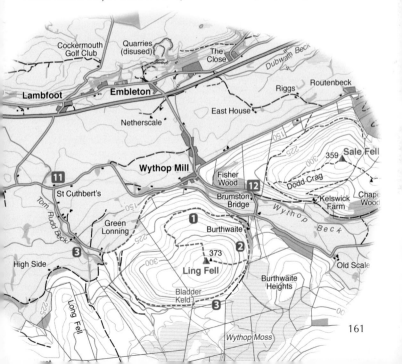

161

Track leading up by the old grouse butts on the northern side

1 Follow the minor road south of the parking area, rising to a T-junction, and here turn right to a gate just past **Burthwaite** leading to a track heading west. Go through and follow the open track onto the green-way as the more regularly worn track sweeps left. Watch to take the left-hand turn uphill from the green-way to the rougher vehicle track in the heather. This climbs easily, and quickly becomes a turf trail. It curves left into a shallow hollow where a line of tumbled stone shooting butts lurks beneath a northern brow. When you reach a fork bear right, and after 150 metres step up the path, right, again to reach the OS column on the summit.

Via the eastern fellside →2km/1¼ miles ↑330m/1080ft ⊕50min

A second popular route which can be combined with Route 1 to provide a compact fell-round

2 Set out with Route **1** to the point where it leaves the road then, at the point where the tracks fork, swing sharp left with the more evidently worn track, duly heading southeast then south beside the fell-bounding fence of **Burthwaite**. Watch for a path leaving the track, breaking up the bank to the right, some 60 metres short of a small red wicket-gate in the fence. This path climbs the eastern fellside through the bracken, then heather, irresistibly aiming towards the summit.

Ascent from Embleton Church 11

Via Tom Rudd Beck →3.6km/2¼ miles ↑260m/850ft ⏱1hr 25min

A roundabout ascent or the outward leg of a pleasing low-level round-trip

3 Walk across the road and follow the confined metalled lane due south, passing some lovely secluded dwellings as you rise beside **Tom Rudd Beck**. At High Side Farm go through the gate and briefly bear up the lane, **Green Lonning**. Soon, on reaching the footpath sign 'Embleton High Common', go through the field-gate and follow the hedge beside burnt gorse to join a track. This leads on by a wall-gate into the Tom Rudd Beck valley. When the track forks keep left, heading straight on and passing a few large quartz boulders. The green track leads to a hurdle-gate. Cross carefully and bear up left, stepping up by several sheep alcoves and an inconsequential spring with a distinctive name – **Bladder Keld**. At this point take a sheep path contouring right through the heather. This leads through a small patch of bracken onto a broad, low-lying grassy plain and joins the track, passing a red wicket-gate to the right. Shortly after, turn left up the fellside with Route **2** for the summit.

Alternatively, for a 6km round-trip, continue down to the road below **Burthwaite**. There turn left to come to the road junction above Wythop Mill then turn left again, looking for the start of **Green Lonning**. A bridleway sign guides onto the quiet byway which rises modestly, with lovely views over the Embleton valley, before it descends to meet the outward leg.

The summit

OS column looking towards Criffel

A fine stone-built OS column stands amid a fragmented bed of heather, alongside a small cairn, some 30 metres to the north, contributed by previous visitors. The best view, of Sale Fell and the Wythop valley backed by the Skiddaw massif, is to be found a little way down the grassy slope to the north, just before it falls into the denser heather.

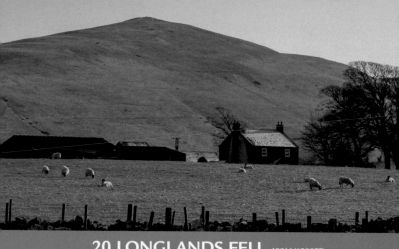

20 LONGLANDS FELL 483M/1585FT

Climb it from	Longlands **26** or Greenhead **27**
Character	A satisfyingly simple ascent
Fell-friendly route	2
Summit grid ref	NY 276 354
Link it with	Great Sca Fell

This elegant little hill lies at the watershed of the Northern Fells, its watercourses draining into the Derwent for the Irish Sea and the Eden for the North Sea round low-lying Aughertree Fell. Despite such a distinction, its generally accepted summit is trumped by higher ground: Lowthwaite Fell, its neighbour to the south, on the ridge connection with Little Sca Fell. This little summit is 26m (85ft) higher but a poorer object of attention and a poorer viewpoint.

A natural stepping-stone en route to Knott, this fell belongs to the hamlet of Longlands, as its name implies. This cluster of houses is still a remote outpost today but a far cry from the humble agricultural settlement noted by Wainwright 60 years ago. The Uldale Fells have only ever hosted one mine, the Longlands Fell copper mine, which operated in the second half of the 19th century but was soon found to be uneconomical and was thus abandoned.

Longlands Fell is the ideal family fell – let granny and grandpa lead your youngsters up it to bag their first mountain-top cairn. They can stroll up just as easily from Longlands (1–2) or Greenhead (3).

↑ *Northern aspect of Longlands Fell from Baggra Yeat*

Ascent from Longlands 26

Via Thwaite → *1.2km/¾ mile* ↑*265m/870ft* ⏱*50min*

A simple direct climb

1 From the gate bear immediately right on the track which fords the gill, branching quickly left up the slope and avoiding the mass of soft rushes and the bracken. A quad track guides half-right up the shallow ridge onto **Thwaite**. The path disappears during the climb and the wide shoulder has nothing but sheep tracks. Leave the bracken behind as you turn east onto the steepening slope and climb doggedly to the summit cairn.

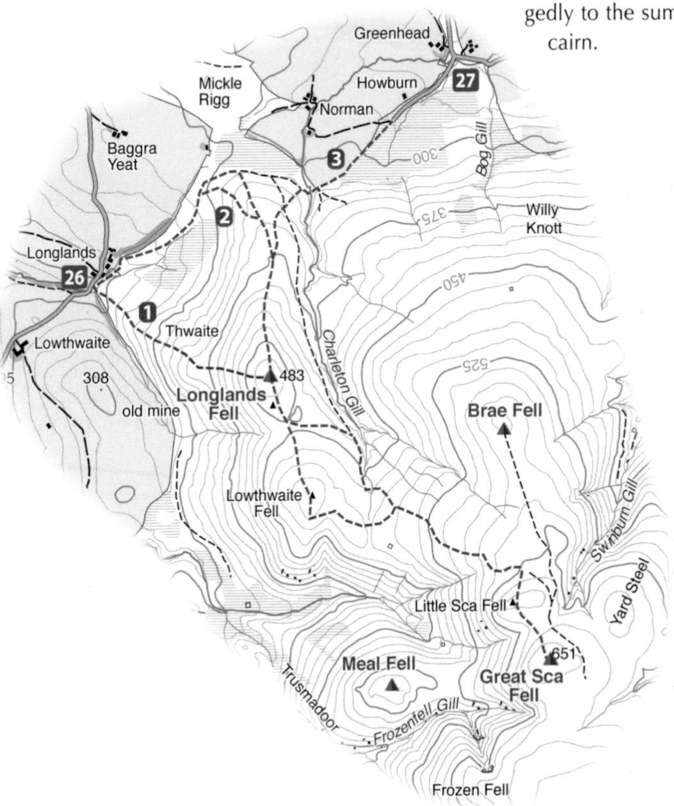

Greenhead

Mickle Rigg

Howburn

27

Norman

3

Baggra Yeat

Bog Gill

300

2

375

Willy Knott

Longlands

26

450

1

Lowthwaite

Thwaite

Charleton Gill

525

305

308

▲483

old mine

Longlands Fell

Brae Fell
▲

Lowthwaite Fell

Little Sca Fell

Swinburn Gill

Yard Steel

▲651

Trusmadoor

Meal Fell
▲

Great Sca Fell

Frozenfell Gill

Frozen Fell

Via the north ridge →*2.1km/1¼ miles* ↑*260m/860ft* ⏱*1hr 10min*

A slightly more circumspect route, an ideal descent from Route 1

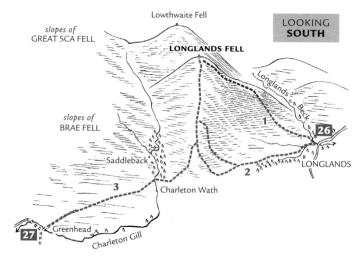

2 Follow the green track from the gate to easily rise above the hamlet of **Longlands**. As the track turns east you can bear off straight up the grassy slope. Alternatively, continue and pass a pit, taking to the fellside short of the waymarked bridleway signed to Great Sca Fell. Climb the simple ridge along a clear path, which runs up the spine due south, to claim your mountain top.

Ascent from Greenhead 27

Over Charleton Gill →*3.5km/2¼ miles* ↑*265m/870ft* ⏱*1hr 25min*

3 Follow the unenclosed road by **Howburn**. When you reach a fork, with the roadway to Norman Farm to the right, go straight ahead along the bridle-track signed 'Public Way, Longlands, Cumbria Way'. This fords **Charleton Gill** at **Charleton Wath**. Just after the gill break off up the bank left with the quad track to cross the bridleway and rise onto the north ridge unimpeded, coming into step with Route **2** to gain the summit.

The summit

Looking to Over Water and Binsey from the summit cairn (photo: Andrew Locking)

The summit has a small cairn, as befits a humble grassy fell-top. The view is most generous in the wide northern arc away from the fells, but you can catch a sneaky glimpse of the fells to the right of Skiddaw, from Crag Hill to Sale Fell.

Safe descents

In poor conditions head N for the north ridge (**2** and **3**) which leads easily down to the old road that links Longlands with Greenhead.

Ridge route

Great Sca Fell →*2.5km/1½ miles* ↓*50m/165ft* ↑*65m/215ft* ⏱*50min*
(→*2.5km/1½ miles* ↓*55m/180ft* ↑*230m/755ft* ⏱*1hr*)
Head S, passing an old shepherds' cairn to reach a pooled depression. Bear left to join the bridleway running up the Charleton Gill valley. Cross the gill to climb SE to the cairn and shelter on Little Sca Fell. The path passes on through another shallow depression to rise onto the broader top of Great Sca Fell. (Alternatively, from the first dip make a beeline S to claim the domed top of Lowthwaite Fell, where a tiny cairn is secreted in the flat-top grassland. The continuing path angles right then switches left (E) to run down the ridge and over a notch to connect with the bridleway.)

21 LONG SIDE 734M/2408FT

Climb it from	Old Sawmill Tearoom 17
Character	Narrow ridge rising irresistibly from Ullock Pike bound for Carl Side
Summit grid ref	NY 248 284
Link it with	Carl Side or Ullock Pike
Part of	The Skiddaw Skyline

Long Side is the name for the central section of the elegant narrow ridge that climbs between Ullock Pike and Carl Side. Sheltering the secretive Southerndale to its north, the little-known northern slopes are dark shadowed, their broken outcrops inhospitable to walkers. Almost as steep but sunny and adorned with heather higher up, the southern slopes do allow one line of approach, following Gable Gill.

The Old Sawmill Tearoom, due west from the summit at the base of Dodd Wood, was a working sawmill until 1970 and was converted into a tearoom in 1981. It is part of the Mirehouse estate. Built in 1666, the main house sits across the A591 amid shady gardens and is perhaps best known for its literary connections. Wordsworth, Tennyson, Southey, Carlyle and Constable were all friends of the Spedding family who have owned it since the 19th century.

↑ *Longside Edge rising to the summit, from above Ullock Pike*

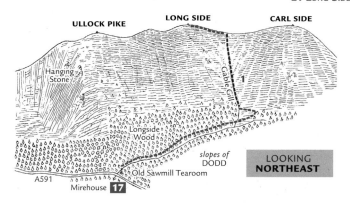

Ascent from Old Sawmill Tearoom 17

Via Gable Gill →*2.8km/1¾ miles* ↑*620m/2040ft* ⏱*1hr 50min*

A tough and seldom-tackled route, but the only worthwhile approach

1 Pass up between the café and toilet block, crossing the footbridge to join and follow the tarmac forest roadway rising on the north side of **Skill Beck**.

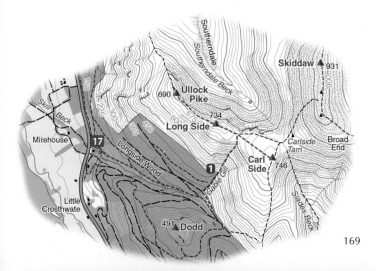

After a clearing make an acute turn left on a track which runs alongside the bounding fence. The diminutive **Gable Gill** spells an end to your casual stroll. Here clamber up the bank and cross the old stile in the fence-corner. Make your way up pathlessly beside the tiny watercourse, amid the moss and heather. Where the forest fence turns left two small ribbons of scree rise ahead – take the left-hand run. There are no hazards and, with a bit of self-belief and dogged persistence, you will slowly make your way ever upward. Reach grass with great relief at the shallow col between Carl Side and Long Side. Turn left to follow the ridge path the short distance to the summit.

The summit

A small cairn sits on a casual comfy perch – a lovely high point on the rising ridge. Most ridge walkers do not break stride to give the summit the attention it deserves. Contemplate the view east to the Helvellyn range and south as far as the Coniston Fells and the Scafells, with a feast of fells crowding in between. Skiddaw's plain slate-streaked slopes curtain off only a comparatively small section of the view to the northeast.

Looking to Skiddaw from the summit

Longside Edge from Broad End

Safe descents

In tricky conditions keep to the ridge. To the SE it leads to Carl Side and from that summit S to Millbeck. Alternatively, take the NW ridge over Ullock Pike, and then after a few easy rock-steps the Edge makes for safe progress for High Side or Ravenstone.

Ridge routes

Carl Side →*0.7km/½ mile* ↓*40m/130ft* ↑*35m/115ft* ⏱*20min*
Head SE and in the shallow depression take the lesser path that breaks half-right from the popular edge path. This leads onto the plateau top and direct to the summit cairn.

Ullock Pike →*0.5km/¼ mile* ↓*60m/195ft* ↑*5m/15ft* ⏱*12min*
Undulating NW, the delightful ridge path is never in doubt – Lakeland ridge-walking at its best. Follow on easily to the summit.

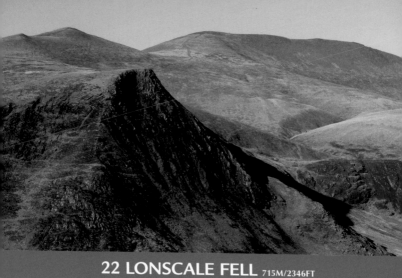

22 LONSCALE FELL 715M/2346FT

Climb it from	Gale Road **5**, Skiddaw House **21** or Blencathra Centre **4**
Character	An awesome scarp and culminating pike on the western side of the Glenderaterra Gap
Fell-friendly route	1
Summit grid ref	NY 285 271
Link it with	Skiddaw Little Man

Lonscale Fell forms the abrupt eastern end of the Skiddaw massif and the western wall of the mighty gorge through which the Glenderaterra runs down to join the River Greta on its way to the Irish Sea. The elegant southern aspect, much admired from the A66, is draped in a shawl of heather. It lures would-be fellwalkers up to savour its ridge-top and cliff-top views down to Keswick and on to Borrowdale, as well as across the gorge east to mighty Blencathra.

Running north to south just under the crags, along the broken eastern declivity, a partially rock-cut bridleway has in recent years been discovered by mountain-bikers, bringing excitement to a new generation. This old gallery was formerly one of the primary means of access to Skiddaw Forest and the lonely Skiddaw House, today a perfectly situated hostel for lovers of peace, solitude and outdoor adventure.

↑ *Lonscale Fell, backed by Skiddaw, from Blease Fell*

Ascents are generally channelled up the southern slopes (1–4) or the blunt northern ridge of Burnt Horse (6). The northeast ridge (5 and 7) is another exciting option, but not one for the faint-hearted.

Ascent from Gale Road 5

Ramblers are invariably tempted to start from the top of Gale Road – but on fair-weather high days and holidays you need to get here early to find a space.

Via Whit Beck →3km/2 miles ↑425m/1400ft ⏱1hr 50min
1 From the hand-gate/stile at the top of Gale Road follow the bridleway left, first with the wall then with the fence, to go through a second hand-gate. Here keep north beside the fence and pass the **Hawell shepherds' memorial**. Ahead the redesigned trail rises above a dip, with the conifer-decorated **Whit Beck** ravine to its right.

At the end of a first great sweeping bend reach a gate beside the platform of a former refreshment hut. Steady zig-zags lead up to where the fence veers right above the beck. Choose whether to follow the fence to the saddle between Lonscale Fell and Jenkin Hill or keep company with the crowd on the main track to where it angles left on the brow and bear back right to the same point. From the saddle go through the hand-gate in the ridge fence and

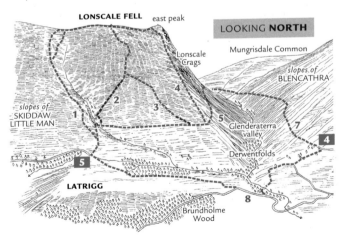

turn right to follow the fence up to a hurdle-gate in the fence-corner, from where a simple trod leads on east-southeast to the summit.

Direct →*2.2km/1½ miles* ↑*430m/1415ft* ⏱*1hr 30min*

The shorter but more pathless of two routes that follow the breast path

2 Start out with Route **1** but fork down right at the **memorial** to ford **Whit Beck**.

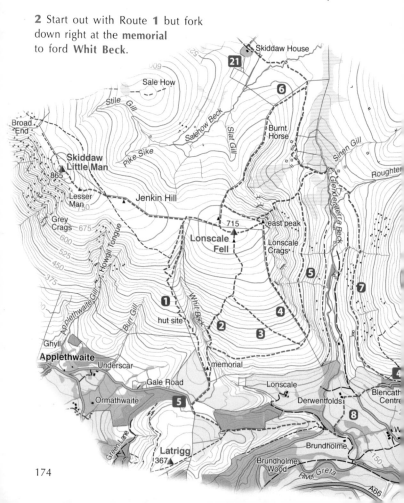

Climb left up the bracken-tangled bank to come alongside a fence above the ravine. A sheep trod aids progress to a large solitary larch tree where a small gill drains off the fell. Follow the course of this shallow gill groove, ascending northeast. Eventually reach the central breast route, where a large tilting post (formerly a gatepost) marks the junction with Route **3**. Head north with a clear path which winds through the heather onto the grassy top and passes the forward cairn to reach the summit.

Up the southeastern slope →3.6km/2¼ miles ↑445m/1460ft ⏲1hr 50min
3 Follow Route **2** to ford **Whit Beck** but then follow the bridleway track, rising easily across the open slope due east. Some 200 metres short of a fence and gate, where you can see a pipe culvert under the track, bear acutely left (northwest) across the pasture to enter the bracken band, and follow a sheep trod through the heather to the tilting post. Turn right to follow Route **2** to the summit.

Via Lonscale Crags →3.8km/2½ miles ↑450m/1475ft ⏲2hr 10min

Straight up the iconic southeastern scarp

4 Follow Route **3** but, instead of turning left up the fell, continue northeast to a gate in the fence running down from the edge of **Lonscale Crags**. Go through this and immediately turn left to accompany the fence up the scarp. The fence-side path climbs a little distance from the edge. Take the opportunity to peer over the brink from time to time. The climb culminates, beyond the fence-corner, on the **east peak** – a fabulous viewpoint with a profound drop beneath your feet. The true summit lies a short distance west.

Via the northeast ridge →4.8km/3 miles ↑525m/1725ft ⏲2hr 30min

The adventurous route

5 From where Route **4** turns up beside the fence, follow the bridletrack on to come onto a rock-cut shelf, impressively high above the Glenderaterra gorge. The track undulates beneath the broken eastern face of **Lonscale Crags** and is quite exposed. After 1.6km (1 mile) spot a path rising to join from the northeast. At this point turn back left and make steady progress up the pathless grassy bank between patches of heather. Reach a shelf and, to your left, find natural access onto the steeper northeast ridge. Keep to the left of the short arête. Progress steadily, passing to the right of the pinnacle – a prominent flake projecting from the ridge. As the invariably damp, slippery rocks (often in shade) become more overbearing find a grassy sheep trod to the left that slants up to the ridge-top of the east peak. From here head west for the true summit.

Rock shelf on the bridleway under Lonscale Crags

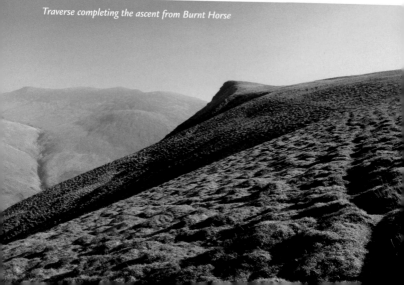

Traverse completing the ascent from Burnt Horse

Ascent from Skiddaw House 21

Via Burnt Horse →*3km/2 miles* ↑*315m/1035ft* ⊕*2hr*

The blunt north ridge is the natural first-thought objective from this starting point.

6 Simply follow the bridleway southeast, crossing the **Salehow Beck** foot-bridge to go through the wall-gate. Rise beside the fence/broken wall onto the crest of **Burnt Horse**. The wall has succumbed to the ravages of the climate on the latter stages of the climb onto this edge, which is beautifully draped with heather. A strong surviving length of wall terminates where the abrupt north slope begins, and only the fence continues to accompany the path to the gateway at the fence-junction. Turn left to reach the summit.

Ascent from Blencathra Centre 4

Via the northeast ridge →*4km/2½ miles* ↑*500m/1640ft* ⊕*2hr 10min*

7 Follow the open track west then north. Ford a minor gill with a fine water-fall, then cross the stone-slab bridge over **Roughten Gill**, pass on by a roof-less shepherd's cot and cross the plank-bridge over **Sinen Gill**. Here the track swings left to skip over a broader plank-bridge spanning the valley headstream and go through a ladder-stile/gate. (The main re-engineered mountain-bikers' trail curves on northwest to link up with Route **6**.) Head up from the gate to take the first path branching left. This contours then rises to cross the lateral track from Gale Road. Climb the facing slope in harmony with Route **5**.

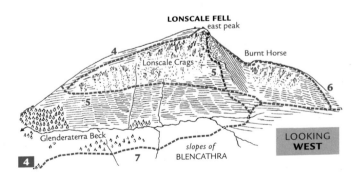

Lonscale Crags from across the Glenderaterra valley

Link from the Blencathra Centre 4 to Gale Road 5

→3.2km/2 miles ↓40m/130ft ↑180m/590ft ⌚1hr

A handy southern connection to the fell which might also be considered, in reverse, after an ascent from the Blencathra Centre by Burnt Horse and a southerly descent to the top of Gale Road.

8 From the car park step back to the cattle grid and go through the hand-gate to its right. Follow the path down to the drive and keep right through the Centre, passing cottage lets, to embark on a footpath signposted to Keswick. The path leads down by a fence to a hand-gate and continues on through conifer woodland via further hand-gates and, latterly, a stile onto the road. Walk down the road to the white-washed **Derwentfolds**. Here go through the gate to its left to follow a lane signposted 'Brundholme', which leads down to a footbridge/ford over **Glenderaterra Beck**. Take a path angling up below a wooded bank to join a road and there turn up right to follow the road as far as a gate. From here follow a track across pasture, with a fence close right, through two further gates to reach the top of Gale Road.

The summit

A cairn marks what may be the highest point, just south of the ridge fence. A tiny cairn some 60 metres further south, with a magnificent view, looks higher but is in fact a fraction lower. Make sure you stand on the east peak to view Skiddaw Forest and the profound gulf fashioned by the Glenderaterra in front of the comparatively blank northern slopes of Blencathra, and the full extent of Roughten Gill to Atkinson Pike.

Safe descents

For Gale Road either follow the fence W (**1**) through the hurdle-gate at the foot of the first descent, go left through the hand-gate and follow the upper course of Whit Beck down to join the engineered trail from Skiddaw, or head E (**4**) towards the east peak and follow the fence right down to the bridleway gate. For Skiddaw House go W to the fence-corner (**6**) and follow the fence N downhill to follow the Burnt Horse ridge.

Ridge route

Skiddaw Little Man →*2.2km/1½ miles* ↓*50m/165ft* ↑*195m/640ft*
⊕*1hr 10min*

Head W and go through the hurdle-gate at the fence-corner, descending to the shallow depression bejewelled with pools. Go through the hand-gate and continue W in harmony with the ridge fence to come up by a cairn on Jenkin Hill. Subsequently cross the popular Skiddaw highway from Gale Road at its stile/gate to zig-zag up the facing fellside onto Lesser Man and rise again to the small domed summit of Little Man.

23 LORD'S SEAT 552M/1811FT

Climb it from	Spout Force **9**, Whinlatter Pass **7**, Powter How **16** or Woodend Brow **15**
Character	A bare summit reached via a conifer-closeted ramble, with the panoramic view a worthy reward
Fell-friendly route	3
Summit grid ref	NY 204 265
Link it with	Barf, Broom Fell or Whinlatter
Part of	The Aiken Beck Horseshoe

Lord of all the fells north of the Whinlatter Pass, this one must always have been popular with visitors to attract its fanciful high-ranking name. Still standing well clear of the surrounding conifers, which have been advancing slowly over the last century, the summit contrasts splendidly with the rest of the range. Four satellite summits make up the massif – Barf, Ullister Hill, Seat How and Aiken.

Whinlatter Forest was some of the very first land to be planted by the Forestry Commission in 1919, but today felling has opened up grand vistas and paths have been created to give leisurely strolls to appeal to the casual visitor. More popular and widely known is the network of Altura trails (specially constructed mountain-bike routes) which have brought life to the plantations, alongside the Go-Ape tree-top experience.

↑ *Lord's Seat in winter raiment, from Darling How plantation*

Naturally enough, forest ways dominate all ascents – some busy, like the two routes up from Whinlatter Pass (3–4), and some peaceful, such as the pair of routes up the Aiken Beck valley (1–2). The route through Beckstones Plantation (5) is steep and the final one, coming in from the north by Beck Wythop (6), is more circumspect in its line of attack.

Ascent from Spout Force 9

Direct →3.6km/2¼ miles ↑330m/1080ft ⏱1hr 15min

1 Follow the forest track from the barrier and keep to the main track until, with a wall coming down to the track from the right and a large larch ahead, you see a footpath waymark post on the left, guiding off the track. Take this path: it runs beside a wall below the track until it naturally drifts down to ford **Aiken Beck**. Follow the ridge, passing to the left of conifers to meet a wall. Bear left here and ford the gill, continuing with the broken wall now on your right until you come to a junction of old walls and there turn right. From here follow a wall running east-southeast to cross one small ford and a fence-stile en route to the top right corner of the plantation. Cross a more substantial fence-stile beside a gate and then walk up the rough pasture on a consistent path to the ridge. Bend left along another fence to join the more regular trail from Whinlatter Forest, which climbs to the summit.

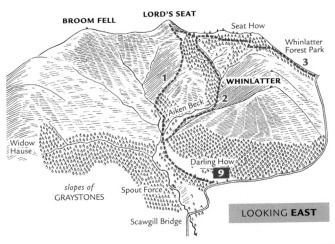

181

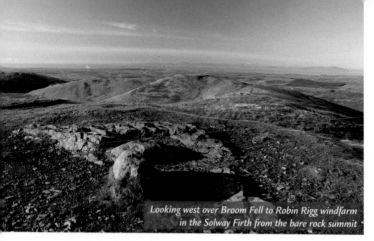

Looking west over Broom Fell to Robin Rigg windfarm in the Solway Firth from the bare rock summit

Via Aiken Beck →*4.4km/2¾ miles* ↑*330m/1080ft* ⏱ *1hr 25min*

A more thorough exploration of the Aiken Beck valley

2 Start out with Route **1**, but instead of turning down to the beck, keep with the main forest track. Follow it higher into the combe, until the track shapes to swing tight right. Here bear off left at the number 24 post. From here a rising footpath moves up a conifer-shaded passage to join the main graded forest path. Follow this left, passing occasional conifers, to a fence-stile and on up to the summit.

Ascent from Whinlatter Pass 7

Direct →*3.2km/2 miles* ↑*235m/770ft* ⏱ *1hr*

The most popular route to the top, almost entirely among conifers

3 Walk down to the road from the parking area and turn right to find the forest track that leaves directly from the barrier at the western edge of the forest. This leads on up, via an exaggerated bend, to a wider track junction (forest post number 3) after just over a kilometre. Here take the right-hand track (green-topped posts), now almost contouring, with a slate exposure to the left of the track. Bend left at the next junction (only Altura bikers go straight on!) and ignore the next green-topped post. Keep to the level track, which becomes a graded path which leads on, round **Ullister Hill**, to a convergence of routes and a fence-stile. Go over this and complete your ascent up the open fell with Route **2**.

183

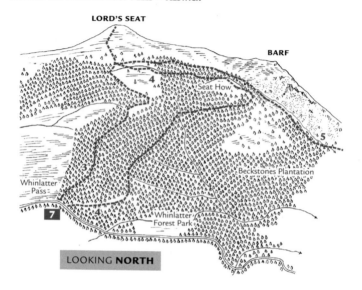

Via Seat How →4km/2½ miles ↑275m/900ft ⏱1hr 25min

This route gives the greatest sense of the drama from the setting of the Forest Park.

4 From the parking area pass on through the main car park and below the **Visitor Centre**. Continue past the Cyclewise shop and up the track, bypassing the barrier and the Altura trails trial area. Carry straight on by forest track junction post number 1, rising steadily up the **Comb Gill** valley and crossing the gill itself. From here follow the track down to a junction. Turn up left, guided by the green-topped post. Watch for the next green-topped post and forest post 54. Here break off the track to the left and follow the graded path winding up into the conifers. This leads steadily up to the bare top of **Seat How**. Backtrack from the top and weave through the conifers of the upper ridge, accompanied by the green-topped posts, on a consistent path. As you come out of the woods, bear right off the made path, following a natural path over the open heather ridge-top and some marshy ground. Meet up with another path merging from the right and, within a few metres, another coming from the left. Here go right to head up to the felltop over the fence-stile with Route **2**.

Ascent from Powter How 16

Via Beckstones Gill →4km/2½ miles ↑475m/1560ft ⏱1hr 30min

Short and sharp and you need to keep your wits about you to navigate.

5 Leave the main road on the byway facing **Swan House**. A footpath sign on the right directs through a kissing-gate and along a birch-woodland way, passing the little white-washed rock known as **the Clerk**. Take this path, which leads over **Beckstones Gill** to a fence-stile and into the plantation. Join the ascending path and avoid being drawn too far right as the steeper woodland is reached. The actual path is the less obvious one, going straight up, which comes onto cleared fellside and winds up to meet a forest track. Climb on with this track, which stays within the trees and rises to swing left and contour to find a made path, acutely right, weaving up to a path-junction. Here go right to cross the fence-stile and climb onto the summit with Route **2**.

Ascent from Woodend Brow 15

Via Wythop Wood →3.6km/2¼ miles ↑495m/1625ft ⏱1hr 40min

A roundabout route from the north, from deepest forestry to open fell

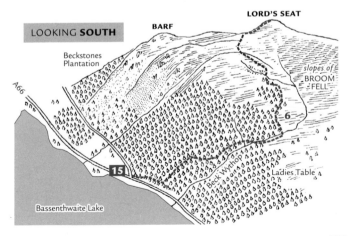

Looking back into the Wythop valley as Route 6 emerges from the forestry

6 Head north with the Beck Wythop road (formerly the main road). After 50 metres reach a footpath sign 'Wythop Hall' on the left and follow this, initially parallel to the roadway. The path steps up onto a forest track but then goes straight over (see the footpath waymark opposite), leading up through the trees with one minor rock-step to reach the same forest track at a higher level. Turn right and follow the track, eventually swinging left after about a kilometre at an open junction. As the track meets a rougher track on the right, branch up this way, with felled plantation on the right. As it becomes more rutted, this track angles up into the conifers of **Hagg** and comes alongside the forest fence. Cross over the tall netting fence at this point onto the open fell and follow the rising ridge (pathless). Curve south to join the ridge path from Barf and head southwest to the summit.

The summit

Apart from the remnants of an old metal fence, with just one strainer post remaining, the summit is quite bare. The view is anything but barren, with a massive all-round panorama to keep you counting the tops for several excited minutes.

Safe descents

Forest tracks ensure a secure line is always available for Whinlatter Pass. Go S then E to the stile and path-junction, then S (**3**) for the swiftest descent. Go SW and then W towards the trees (**1**) for an equally secure route to the Aiken Beck valley and Spout Force.

Ridge routes

Barf → 1.2km/¾ mile ↓130m/425ft ↑45m/150ft ☺30min
A strong path leads off NE and during the descent curves E as it moves through marshy hollows to rise, dry again, onto the open summit.

Broom Fell → 1.6km/1 mile ↓70m/230ft ↑30m/100ft ☺35min
Leave the summit in a NW direction. After the initial bank the ridge is quite level, with two cross-ridge fences to negotiate via stiles in order to reach the tall summit currick.

Whinlatter → 3.6km/2¼ miles ↓90m/295ft ↑55m/180ft ☺1hr
Follow the main path S and cross the fence-stile into the open woodland randomly dotted with self-sown conifers. Follow the made path, keeping S at the path-junction. This path becomes a track and, after swinging right, comes to an unusually wide junction. Keep right only for a few paces, and where the Altura trail slips into the forest, left, find a path immediately to its left. This leads on and over a section of the trail (be watchful for careering bikers) and rises to a hand-gate in a fence-corner. Go through and, keeping the fence close left, follow on SW, with some wet patches, to join the ridge. Bear W to cross Whinlatter Top (the true summit) and continue via a wall-gap to the accepted summit with its shelter.

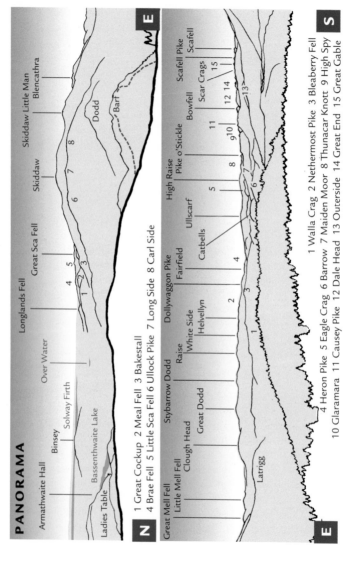

PANORAMA

E

Armathwaite Hall
Binsey
Solway Firth
Over Water
Longlands Fell
Great Sca Fell
Skiddaw
Skiddaw Little Man
Blencathra
Dodd
Barf
Bassenthwaite Lake
Ladies Table

N

1 Great Cockup 2 Meal Fell 3 Bakestall
4 Brae Fell 5 Little Sca Fell 6 Ullock Pike 7 Long Side 8 Carl Side

S

Great Mell Fell
Little Mell Fell
Clough Head
Great Dodd
Stybarrow Dodd
Raise
White Side
Helvellyn
Dollywaggon Pike
Fairfield
Catbells
Ullscarf
High Raise
Pike o'Stickle
Bowfell
Scar Crags
Scafell Pike
Scafell
Latrigg

E

1 Walla Crag 2 Nethermost Pike 3 Bleaberry Fell
4 Heron Pike 5 Eagle Crag 6 Barrow 7 Maiden Moor 8 Thunacar Knott 9 High Spy
10 Glaramara 11 Causey Pike 12 Dale Head 13 Outerside 14 Great End 15 Great Gable

PANORAMA

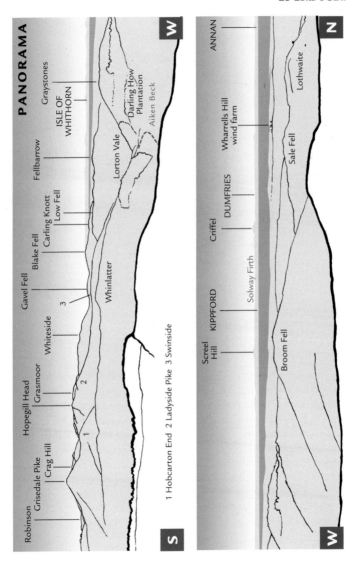

W

Graystones

ISLE OF
WHITHORN

Fellbarrow

Darling How
Plantation

Aiken Beck

Lorton Vale

Carling Knott
Low Fell

Blake Fell

Gavel Fell

3

Whinlatter

Whiteside

Hopegill Head
Grasmoor

2

Griesdale Pike
Crag Hill

1

Robinson

S

1 Hobcarton End 2 Ladyside Pike 3 Swinside

N

ANNAN

Lothwaite

Wharrells Hill
wind farm

Criffel

DUMFRIES

Sale Fell

Solway Firth

Screel
Hill KIPPFORD

Broom Fell

W

189

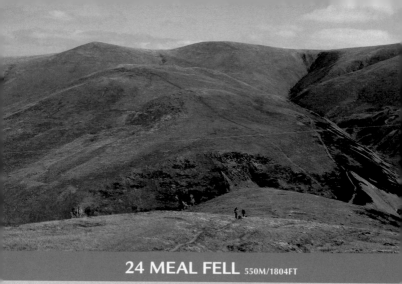

24 MEAL FELL 550M/1804FT

Climb it from	Horsemoor Hills **22** or Longlands **26**
Character	Tucked away above Trusmadoor, a shy little height forming a handy bridge between grassy fells
Fell-friendly route	3
Summit grid ref	NY 282 337
Link it with	Great Cockup or Great Sca Fell

Shy Meal Fell hides in the warm embrace of the satellite ridges to the west of Knott, between Great Sca Fell and Great Cockup. Its only distinction being that it forms the eastern flank of the scenic glacial gap of Trusmadoor, for most walkers it is little more than a stop on a greater circuit of the Uldale Fells, but no matter.

For all its modest proportions this is a lovely fell to discover. On its sequestered summit you can imagine yourself far removed from life's turmoil – a timeless air pervades the setting, and only vapour trails in the sky give a clue to a global world of travel and travail. If views of the Solway and the distant Galloway Hills are to your liking, this little belvedere will fit the bill.

Low-level routes lead in round neighbouring fells to the west and the north, rising to the ridge from either side, and pairing up to make fine and most likely solitary fell days.

↑ *Meal Fell from Great Cockup, looking over Trusmadoor,*
with Great Sca Fell forming the horizon

Ascent from Horsemoor Hills 22

A pair of routes making a neat circuit of Little Cockup, Route 2 the more watery line

Via Burntod Gill → 4.2km/2½ miles ↑365m/1200ft ⊙ 1hr 35min

1 Walk north to the farm track that leaves the minor road between Orthwaite and Horsemoor Hills. Step off left 100 metres beyond the second quarry on a lovely turf trail signed 'Burn Tod'. This rises onto the little eminence above the unseen **Brockle Crag** and continues east until the slope begins to fall. Here veer half-left with a strong sheep path which wades through the bracken. When it reaches the heather the path improves as it runs into the valley of **Burntod Gill**, well above the ravine. Press on to reach the exciting gap of **Trusmadoor** – the ideal place for an ambush. Either follow the more obvious shepherds' drove running above **Frozenfell Gill** to the saddle to the east of the fell and backtrack west, or climb northeast, making a beeline for the felltop.

Via the Ellen gorge → 4.8km/3 miles ↑390m/1280ft ⊙ 1hr 45min

2 From the gate off the road turn abruptly left up beside the intake wall on a quad track. This largely contours, sweeping round Orthwaite Bank and on

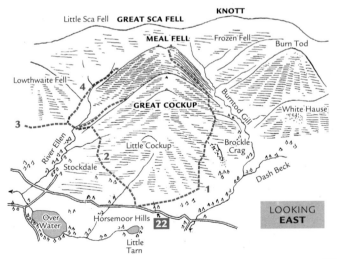

beneath the tiny eminence of **Little Cockup** to ford **Dale Gill**, keeping above the mire draining into the Ellen gorge. As the track comes closer to the **River Ellen** boggy ground is difficult to avoid, and it is easy to lose the path before reaching the main ford beside a fold. From here tramp north to find dry ground along the bracken fringe at the foot of Lowthwaite Fell, and there pick up a path leading east to another ford. Cross and follow the broadening tongue, passing a large sheepfold, into the head of the valley. As the slope steepens bend back right (southwest) on a shelf-path which leads to the broad saddle and joins the ridge path leading due west up to the summit.

Ascent from Longlands 26

The beeline route up to scenic Trusmadoor, with a variant line tracing the headwaters of the River Ellen

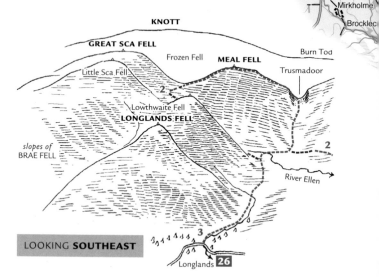

LOOKING **SOUTHEAST**

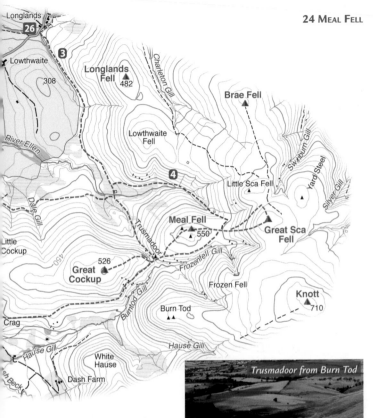

Trusmadoor from Burn Tod

Via Trusmadoor → *3.4km/2 miles*
↑ *345m/1210ft* ⏲ *1hr 15min*
3 Go through the gate and at once bear right off the green track. Ford the beck and continue on a track which leads south, close beside a wall, above Longlands Beck. Pass below the spoil of a sealed mine, and after a ruined timber shed pursue the green track to ford the infant **River Ellen**. The path leads

up beside the glacial esker ridge to draw into and through the **Trusmadoor** gap. After a cairn at the top bear up left on a modest path which leads naturally to the summit.

Via Ellen Head →*3.7km/2¼ miles* ↑*340m/1115ft* ⏱*1hr 20min*
4 Follow Route **3** as far as the marshy ground approaching the ford of the **River Ellen**. Here turn left to pick out an eastward-bearing path and join Route **2** to reach the summit.

The summit

Most visitors consider the sizeable shelter as the summit, and it certainly has character and a sense of being on top. But the precise summit, marked by a humbler cairn, lies on the parallel ridge-top to the north, beyond the pool-jewelled hollow.

Cairn on the west top

Safe descents

Head SW for Trusmadoor, where there are two options. Traverse the heathery slopes of Great Cockup above Burntod Gill to the SW (**1**) – the path is little better than a sheep trod until the bridleway running over the shoulder above Brockle Crag is joined. Alternatively, head NW for Longlands (**3**) – the path is far more tangible, with the boggy ground after the Ellen ford the only discomfort.

Ridge routes

Great Cockup →*1.2km/¾ mile* ↓*110m/360ft* ↑*85m/280ft* ⊕*35min*
Descend SW into Trusmadoor, pass the cairn and continue up the northwest edge onto the ridge, drifting SW to the small cairn in an ocean of grass, all with the aid of a continuous path.

Great Sca Fell →*0.9km/½ mile* ↓*25m/80ft* ↑*130m/430ft* ⊕*25min*
Follow the natural drift of the ridge E down through the wide depression, and a consistent path begins to climb. At the fork either hold to the leading west ridge all the way to the summit or opt for the left-hand path, which comes to the saddle between Great and Little Sca Fell, from where the ridge path leads S to the summit cairn.

25 SALE FELL 359M/1178FT

Climb it from	Woodend Brow **15**, Pheasant Hotel **14**, Wythop Church **13** or Brumston Bridge **12**
Character	A popular grassy romp for joggers and dog-walkers, flanked by old woodland and a little gorse
Fell-friendly route	6
Summit grid ref	NY 194 297

It is hard to tire of characterful little Sale Fell. With its near neighbour Ling Fell, it shelters the pastoral valley of Wythop to the west. Bounded to the east and north by Bassenthwaite Lake and Embleton vale, it is cut off from the Lord's Seat massif by the confusingly named Wythop Beck and Beck Wythop. Between these two, Wythop valley has an enduring peace about it, with its native oakwood and the mighty scree slopes of Skiddaw the dramatic backdrop.

A host of historic features add interest hereabouts. Opposite the Pheasant Hotel at Dubwath, a low-set wooded mound is crowned by the Iron Age hillfort Castle How. The name of nearby Peel Wyke, meaning 'the stronghold bay', derives from this hillfort site. Peel Wyke was also the scene of the very first sailing regatta in the Lake District, established in the 1780s by Joseph Pocklington, who built the house on Derwent Island on Derwentwater. Chapel Wood hides another ancient secret, the remains of Old Wythop Church, built in the 14th century and

↑ *Sale Fell from Ling Fell*

abandoned in the 1860s, and still the site of an open-air service every August, and Wythop Wood a quiet memorial seat for Wilfred Watson, with a lovely view over the lake to Dodd.

Sample the forest scarp by following any of the first three routes or engage with its more open aspects, from the north and the west, on the subsequent five.

Ascent from Woodend Brow 15

Start from here to make the most of Thornthwaite Wood and lovely Bassenthwaite Lake on your way to the summit.

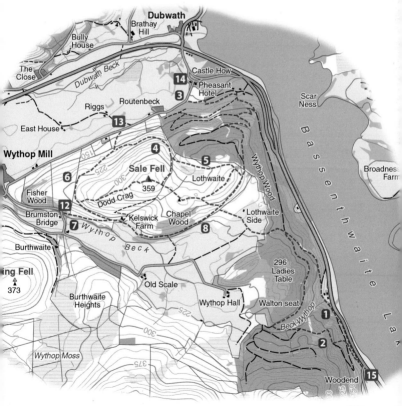

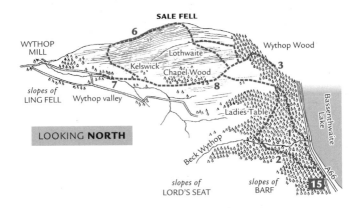

SALE FELL

WYTHOP
MILL

Wythop Wood

Lothwaite

Kelswick

Chapel Wood

slopes of
LING FELL

Wythop valley

Ladies Table

Bassenthwaite Lake

Beck Wythop

LOOKING **NORTH**

slopes of
LORD'S SEAT

slopes of
BARF

A66

Via Lothwaite →*4km/2½ miles* ↑*350m/1150ft* ⏱ *1hr 30min*

1 Follow the old road leading on northwest beside the main road, signed as a cycleway. Keep with this to the turning circle and entry off the A66 at **Beck Wythop**. Pass above the cottages, leaving the truncated road to go up the cycle trail as it rises through the felled conifers to cross a forest track.

 2 Alternatively, reach the forest track by following the footpath signed 'Wythop Hall' off the old road after a matter of 70 metres. Step over the forest

Rigg and furrow on the high shoulder of the fell south of the summit

track at your first encounter with it and head up the woodland slope to join it higher up near a scenic bend. Keep to the track, looking for a short flight of steps on the right after some 400 metres. Take these to follow the path to a footbridge over **Beck Wythop**. Rise on through the wood to meet a further forest track, and turn right with this. Keep to the forest track until, after a slight descent, it encounters a crossing bridleway and Route **1**.

The bridleway winds up on bedrock to reach a gate/stile into pasture. Here your continuing field-edge track leads on by gates, passing the derelict **Lothwaite Side** and a line of gangly thorns, to meet a track at a gate. Go right, rising briefly, then turn left up the bracken-bank path leading over the brow. Pass a cairn on your left en route to a wall-gate. Go through this to climb on up to the summit.

Ascent from the Pheasant Hotel 14

Via Wythop Wood →*3.2km/2 miles* ↑*340m/1115ft* ⏱*1hr 25min*

Follow the forest switchbacks with care to reach the open fell.

3 Follow the back road south from the hotel junction. Continue up the hill a little further, and just before the first house in **Routenbeck** turn left at the sign-posted footpath (with seat and red-squirrel sign). The path gently rises through the mature forest, coming above the timber-built Forestry Commission office buildings and forestry yard. Continue round the hill to take the next acute

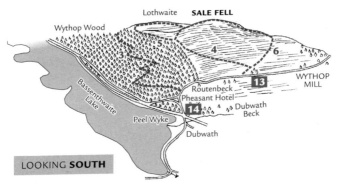

LOOKING **SOUTH**

turn up right. At the top turn acutely left, and then right, and finally take a left turn. When this too comes to a junction, continue forward to a gate out of the forestry. Once out on the drove-way there are two clear-cut options. Bear up right after 100 metres on a path which brushes under oak trees to gain the brow and then turns left along the scarp top of **Lothwaite**. Alternatively, continue along the green-way to find a path slanting up to the right (in common with Route **1**). Proceed with Route **1** via the small cairn to the summit.

Ascent from Wythop Church 13

Via the northern slopes →2.4km/1½ miles ↑210m/690ft ⏱1hr

Choose between a direct ascent and a sweeping tour of the high ground.

4 From the church parking area take the green-way slanting up and through a gateway. Here turn left with a well-graded grass track which leads up to a gate. However, instead of marching through, turn right, keeping the wall close left. Come up by a second gate on top of the ridge and bear right with the path onto the summit. **5** Alternatively, go through the second gate to follow the path running east, parallel to the forest-bounding wall, with some marshy ground, to gain the scarp edge of **Lothwaite**. Turn right along this crest and follow on until you meet the ascending path. Here turn right to join Routes **1** and **2** and follow them to the summit.

Via Dodd Crag →2km/1¼ miles ↑200m/655ft ⏱50min
6 Take the green-way and, from the gateway above the church, keep right, following it on to ease up and cross the shoulder of the fell beside the wall. Here branch up east onto the ridge, following a path which climbs the western ridge above **Dodd Crag** past quartz boulders to the summit.

Ascent from Brumston Bridge 12

Two much-loved Sunday strolls, even better in combination

Via Kelswick →1.6km/1 mile ↑210m/690ft ⏱45min
7 Follow the road leading up east from the parking area via a gate up to **Kelswick Farm**. Just short of the buildings take a terrace path leading sharply

Outcrop near the summit, looking to Ling Fell

back left, contouring past a seat to meet the wall on the ridge-end. Here bear up right to join Route **6** to the summit.

Via Chapel Wood →*3.2km/2 miles* ↑*210m/690ft* ⏰*1hr 10min*
8 Follow the road east from the parking area to **Kelswick Farm** and carry on, along the gated track beyond, passing a curious rectangular wall structure, Old Wythop Church. Pass on through the base of **Chapel Wood**, protected by a deer-fence, pitching up acutely left above **Lothwaite Side** to join Route **1** and follow it to the summit.

The summit

A large convex slate exposure is the only feature of note on a cairnless crest. The view is concentrated on Skiddaw and its immediate satellites. Elsewhere, intervening fellsides block out much of stirring merit, although the Helvellyn range forms a considerable eastern horizon.

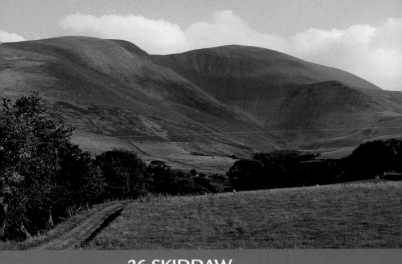

26 SKIDDAW 931M/3054FT

Climb it from	Gale Road **5**, Millbeck **6**, Rabbit Warren **18**, High Side **19**, Peter House **20** or Skiddaw House **21**
Character	Iconic presence to the north of Keswick, simple in form and magnificent in scale
Fell-friendly route	10
Summit grid ref	NY 260 291
Link it with	Bakestall, Carl Side or Skiddaw Little Man
Part of	The Skiddaw Skyline

Skiddaw (traditionally pronounced 'skidda'), the patriarch in the family portrait of the Northern Fells, provides a perfect backdrop to the town of Keswick and all views north over Derwentwater. This much-loved mountain is the fourth highest in Lakeland – indeed, going north, one has to travel 200km to match its grandeur in Scotland, with Ben Lomond standing at 974m/3195ft. It's also on most fellwalkers' bucket lists – and within most visitors' attainment thanks to the well-worn path from Gale Road.

Behind to its northeast lies Skiddaw House, sitting on the 470m/1550ft contour in the Caldew basin. The present hostel is quite the perfect haven from which to explore this enchanting fell country. Tailor-made for outdoor enthusiasts, it is much enjoyed by C2C bikers and Cumbria Way walkers, but it is

↑ *Skiddaw and Barkbethdale, seen from Bassenthwaite Village* also the ideal base for anyone set on a thorough exploration of the Northern Fells – the long march in a key part of the whole magical experience.

The standard ascent of Skiddaw from the top of Gale Road (1) is nothing more than a steady plod, although you could always add one of the district's best viewpoints, Skiddaw Little Man, to the return journey. Routes to the top exist around the compass, none without merit, but top billing goes to Longside Edge (3–4).

Ascent from Gale Road 5 *off map S*

Direct →*5.2km/3¼ miles* ↑*640m/2060ft* ⏲*2hr 30min*

A stairway to heaven

1 From the hand-gate/stile at the top of Gale Road follow the bridleway left with the wall, and then the fence, to go through a second hand-gate. Here keep north beside the fence, passing the Skiddaw shepherds' **memorial.**

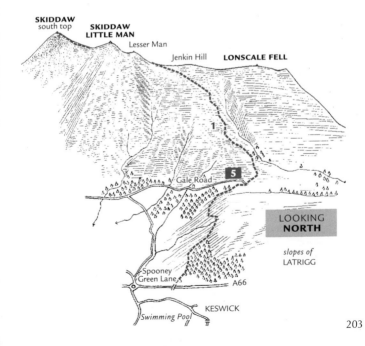

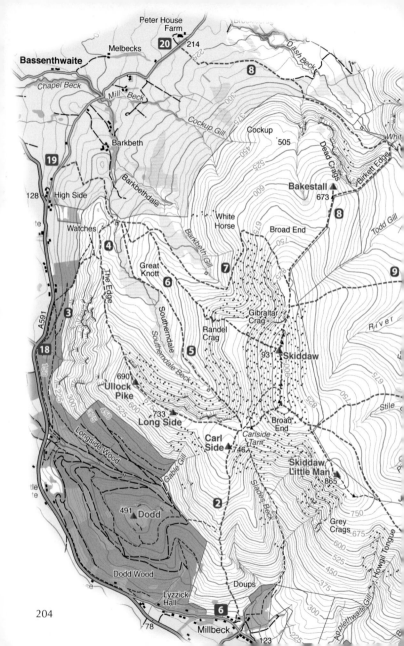

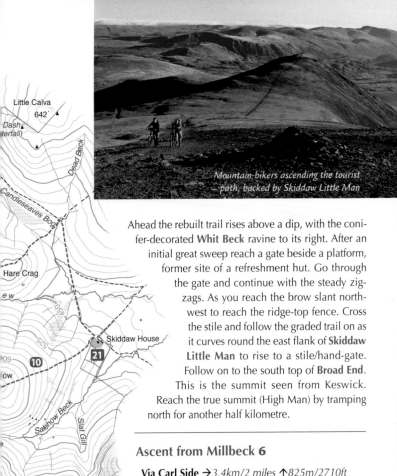

Mountain-bikers ascending the tourist path, backed by Skiddaw Little Man

Ahead the rebuilt trail rises above a dip, with the conifer-decorated **Whit Beck** ravine to its right. After an initial great sweep reach a gate beside a platform, former site of a refreshment hut. Go through the gate and continue with the steady zigzags. As you reach the brow slant northwest to reach the ridge-top fence. Cross the stile and follow the graded trail on as it curves round the east flank of **Skiddaw Little Man** to rise to a stile/hand-gate. Follow on to the south top of **Broad End**. This is the summit seen from Keswick. Reach the true summit (High Man) by tramping north for another half kilometre.

Ascent from Millbeck 6

Via Carl Side →*3.4km/2 miles* ↑*825m/2710ft* ⏱*2hr 20min*

The route that replaced the once-popular struggle up Slades Beck

2 A footpath signed 'Skiddaw' departs from the access lane to Ben-y-Craig and continues up a

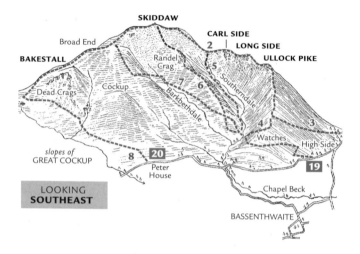

confined passage through kissing-gates. Emerge to join a turf path sweeping left up the fell, uninhibited by bracken. Cross a fence-stile en route to the first high brow. Follow the regular path as it slants up the heather slope

Longside Edge from the direct ascent path onto the south top

to the summit of **Carl Side**. The path runs over the top and down to Carlside Col, with its seasonal pool. Here most folk fork left but the smart choice is to head for **Broad End** – a path leads from a cairn off to the right of the regular way, winding northeast up to the south-top cairn. Head north to claim the true summit.

Ascent from Rabbit Warren 18

Via the Edge →5.2km/3¼ miles ↑845m/2775ft ⏱2hr 30min

A sideways approach to a royal ridge route

3 From the car park go right and quickly meet a path leading left (northeast). Follow this, with felled plantation to the left, to reach a hand-gate, where a more direct footpath from Ravenstone converges. Head up with the fence on your left and soon take a footpath that breaks up right to gain the ridge. Turn right to climb **the Edge**, only latterly encountering any rock obstacles, all easily negotiated, to reach **Ullock Pike**. From here on the ridge is something of a rollercoaster, quite chiselled, and a hugely impressive fellwalking experience. Having climbed over **Long Side** the primary path keeps to the brink of Southerndale to reach Carlside Col and link up with Route **2**, crossing to **Broad End** and on to the summit.

Ascent from High Side 19

Via the Edge →5.5km/3½ miles ↑820m/2690ft ⏱2hr 45min

4 Go through the gate/stile from the layby and bear half-left with the track, rising beside the gorse. Where this ends bend right beside the old hedge-line, and where this in turn ends follow the trace of a track which switches up left to a gate, then traverses a field to a gate/ladder-stile. The green track thus comes over the ridge pasture and swings right above **Southerndale Beck**. Leading on by a stile/gate along the shelf, it duly arrives at a broad plank-bridge over the beck, beside a twin-roomed sheepfold. Step off the track right and follow the green path as it slants up to **Watches**, an odd assemblage of igneous rocks. The ridge path switches up delightfully among the heather to unite with Route **3**.

Via Southerndale →5km/3 miles ↑780m/2560ft ⏱2hr 30min

A peaceful valley approach

5 Set off with Route **4** as far as the broad plank-bridge spanning **Southerndale Beck**. Here stride forward to cross the bridge and quickly turn right onto a grass track which keeps above the marshy dale bottom. This runs on consistently, crossing two patches of heather to reach the dale head. The path is promptly lost but the slope ahead is a straightforward if steady climb, avoiding stony scree, to Carlside Col, where it links with Route **2**.

Via Randel Crag →3.7km/2¼ miles ↑770m/2530ft ⏱2hr 15min

A seldom-trod ridge and the only direct approach to the true summit

6 Reach the Southerndale Beck footbridge with Route **4** but then head east on the clear path, which rises onto the near headland of Little Knott and keeps to the undulating high ground over **Great Knott** and Buzzard Knott. As the ridge steepens keep to the right of the stony slope of

Broad End (north top) from Randel Crag

Randel Crag. The path fades as it crosses the grassy alp, passing a W-shaped pool, to take on the slate slope of Skiddaw. There is no sure path, but neither is there any obstacle to deflect you from forging steadily on to the summit.

Via Barkbethdale →7.3km/4½ miles ↑790m/2590ft ⏱2hr 45min

A non-standard route to the top, switchbacking across the northwestern slopes

7 Reach the Southerndale Beck footbridge with Route **4**, then take the line half-right beyond the first dale trail to run over the Low Knott ridge into upper **Barkbethdale**. This path comes to a natural turning point beneath the scree-streaked dalehead, with evidence of a stone extraction path leading up a little way. Ignore this and swing left (north-northeast) on a pronounced sheep trod. This climbs steadily onto the heather of **White Horse**. Reach a cross-paths. From here follow the continuing path up the slope east then southeast onto **Broad End**. The path is briefly lost as you come onto the plateau but you can soon join the ridge path from Bakestall, turning south to claim the summit.

Ascent from Peter House 20

Via Bakestall →*6km/3¾ miles* ↑*730m/2400ft* ⏱*3hr*

The classic approach from the north

8 Follow the gated road towards Whitewater Dash and Skiddaw House. Step off the metalled road as a track forks right, with a stone indicating 'Bridleway via Dash Falls, Skiddaw House, Threlkeld'. After the next gate follow the open track as it runs on beneath the cliffs of **Dead Crags**, offering views of the elegant embowered waterfall of Whitewater Dash half-left. The track climbs to a gate. Don't go through this but step off right and walk steeply up beside the fence as it climbs **Birkett Edge**. Mount steadily to a cairn at the left-hand angle of the fence and continue to follow the fence-side path. Eventually the fence drifts away as it climbs onto the broad plateau of **Broad End**, ahead of the final short pull onto the north top. Join with Route **7**, heading south to the summit.

Ascent from Skiddaw House 21

Via Hare Crag →*4.6km/3 miles* ↑*515m/1690ft* ⏱*2hr 20min*

A path created by runners on the Bob Graham Round heading off Skiddaw to scoop up Great Calva

9 Follow the supply track north as far as the lone hawthorn bush beside the **Dead Beck** culvert. The path sets off beside the stream, but as the beck turns south it trends southwest, treading the spongy heather vegetation of **Candleseaves Bog** to reach the dry bank of the **Hare Crag** ridge. Search in

Skiddaw House independent hostel

vain for a crag, but notice a large ruined sheepfold and, adjacent, a small drystone shooting butt. The path draws over the ridge onto leveller ground, with one small mossy hollow to cross before a good grass trail sets to work climbing the long slope due almost west. Progress is rapid up the comparatively easy-angled grass slope. Reach the plain fence and step over carefully. Turn left to join Route **7** and the ridge path to the summit.

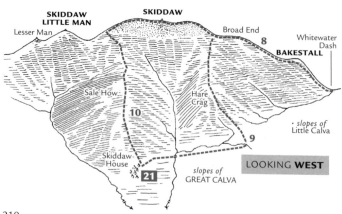

Via Sale How →*3.6km/2¼ miles* ↑*480m/1575ft* ⏱*2hr 15min*

10 From the access gate turn up left, heading southwest from the bedraggled copse enclosure onto the damp heather-decked ridge. The top of **Sale How** has a certain individuality and deserves a moment's pause and appreciation. The path dips through a shallow damp patch before completing a grassy climb to the hand-gate/stile in the fence that runs under the eastern scree slopes of Skiddaw. Now join the popular path from Keswick (Route **1**) to the south-top cairn and on to the summit.

The summit

The summit ridge of fractured slate is an exalted promenade some 700 metres long. Inevitably there are several cairns and low shelters angled for protection from prevailing westerlies. The largest shelter rests close to High Man, the summit, which is marked by a stout OS column with its concrete base resting like a raft on the bare ground. A few paces west stands a cylindrical

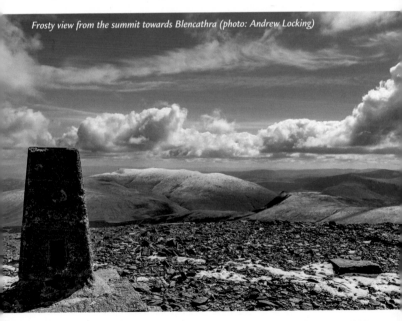

Frosty view from the summit towards Blencathra (photo: Andrew Locking)

Skiddaw from Blease Fell

topograph offering visitors an idea of what can be seen on a good day. A little distance below there is another shelter, frequented by seekers of solitude. In good visibility the views are indeed stunning. For the best view of Lakeland stand at the south top, and for Scotland, panning the Solway, stand at the north top. You'll probably have these places largely to yourself.

Safe descents

The primary routes of ascent give confidence and security in poor conditions. The safest are from the south top: head SE (**1**) for Keswick or NE then ENE to Skiddaw House (**9**) or, after the steepish descent, SW to Carlside Col for Millbeck (**2**). For the Dash valley go N from the north top to find the fence (**8**) – a sure guide down Birkett Edge to the Skiddaw House supply track.

Ridge routes

Bakestall →2km/1¼ miles ↓270m/890ft ↑10m/35ft ⊕35min
Head N to the north-top cairn then follow the ridge path down onto the plateau of Broad End to come by the plain wired fence. Follow this down to a

saddle, passing a bield and, at the fence-corner, a cairn. Here veer half-left to the summit cairn.

Carl Side →*1.3km/¾ mile* ↓*210m/695ft* ↑*30m/100ft* ⏲*30min*
Follow the spine of the ridge S. The more popular route veers W from the second shelter down the awkward slate slope. The true ridge is better and persists to the cairn of the south top, heading SW down the nose of Broad End. In both cases a regular path ensures arrival in the saddle of Carlside Col. Pass the cairn and attain the summit SSW up the easy rise.

Skiddaw Little Man →*1.6km/1 mile* ↓*125m/410ft* ↑*60m/195ft* ⏲*45min*
Follow the roof of the summit ridge S to the cairn on the south top. Head left (SE) down the popular trail, and short of the fence hand-gate/stile fork right on the clear path. This comes down to join the fence as it heads through the depression, then climbs on, quickly unshackling itself from the fence, to reach the summit cairn.

Skiddaw Little Man from Carl Side

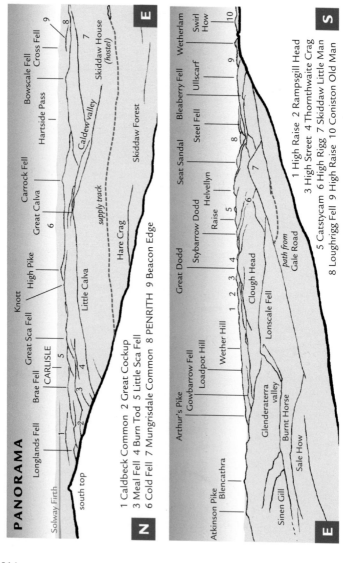

PANORAMA

E

Cross Fell
Bowscale Fell
Hartside Pass
Carrock Fell
Skiddaw House (hostel)
Great Calva
Caldew valley
Skiddaw Forest
High Pike
Knott
Great Sca Fell
Hare Crag
supply track
Little Calva
Brae Fell
CARLISLE
Longlands Fell
south top
Solway Firth

N

1 Caldbeck Common 2 Great Cockup
3 Meal Fell 4 Burn Tod 5 Little Sca Fell
6 Cold Fell 7 Mungrisdale Common 8 PENRITH 9 Beacon Edge

S

Swirl How
Wetherlam
Bleaberry Fell
Ullscarf
Steel Fell
Seat Sandal
Helvellyn
Stybarrow Dodd
Raise
Great Dodd
Clough Head
Lonscale Fell
path from Gale Road
Wether Hill
Loadpot Hill
Gowbarrow Fell
Arthur's Pike
Glenderaterra valley
Burnt Horse
Sale How
Sinen Gill
Atkinson Pike
Blencathra

E

1 High Raise 2 Rampsgill Head
3 High Street 4 Thornthwaite Crag
5 Catstycam 6 High Rigg 7 Skiddaw Little Man
8 Loughrigg Fell 9 High Raise 10 Coniston Old Man

PANORAMA

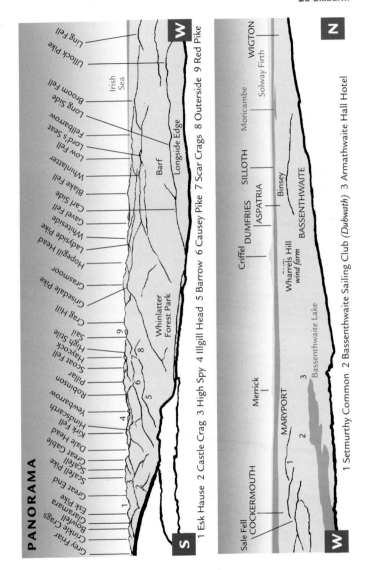

S — Grey Friar, Crinkle Crags, Bowfell, Glaramara, Esk Pike, Great End, Scafell Pike, Scafell, Great Gable, Dale Head, Kirk Fell, Hindscarth, Yewbarrow, Robinson, Pillar, Scoat Fell, Haycock, High Stile, Sail, Crag Hill, Grisedale Pike, Grasmoor, Hopegill Head, Ladyside Pike, Whiteside, Gavel Fell, Carl Side, Blake Fell, Whinlatter, Low Fell, Lord's Seat, Fellbarrow, Long Side, Broom Fell, Ullock Pike, Ling Fell, Whinlatter Forest Park, Barf, Longside Edge, Irish Sea

W

1 Esk Hause 2 Castle Crag 3 High Spy 4 Ilgill Head 5 Barrow 6 Causey Pike 7 Scar Crags 8 Outerside 9 Red Pike

N — Sale Fell, COCKERMOUTH, Merrick, MARYPORT, Criffel, DUMFRIES, SILLOTH, ASPATRIA, WIGTON, Moricambe, Solway Firth, Binsey, Wharrels Hill wind farm, BASSENTHWAITE, Bassenthwaite Lake

W

1 Setmurthy Common 2 Bassenthwaite Sailing Club (*Dubwath*) 3 Armathwaite Hall Hotel

215

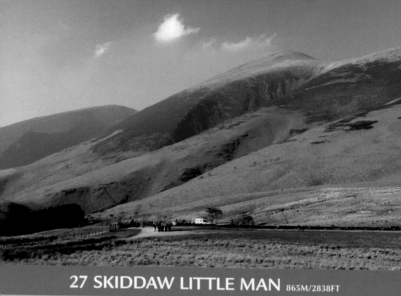

27 SKIDDAW LITTLE MAN 865M/2838FT

Climb it from	Gale Road **5**, Millbeck **6** or Skiddaw House **21**
Character	Outlier of Skiddaw, renowned for its peerless view down Derwentwater into the mountainous heart of Lakeland
Fell-friendly route	6
Summit grid ref	NY 267 278
Link it with	Lonscale Fell or Skiddaw

Skiddaw's imposing southern outlier, Skiddaw Little Man is just far enough away from its higher neighbour to have a distinctive character all its own. Eclipsing the main summit from some angles, it has a tremendous presence and offers its own fell adventures. Undoubtedly, the real highlight is the view – the most complete panorama of Lakeland fells from any Lakeland summit.

Signs of the past lie on many of the ascent routes. The tangle of rusting fence posts at the summit cairn contains remnants of a long-removed Victorian ridge fence. The metal railings above the weir beside Slades Beck date back to the former waterworks, and the fox bield between Skiddaw and Little Man recalls the glory days of the Blencathra Foxhounds in the mid-19th century. Last but not least, just up from Gale Road on Route 1, the inscription on the shepherds' memorial is self-explanatory.

216   ↑ *Skiddaw Little Man, with Grey Crags centre stage, from Gale Road*

The most straightforward route is up from Gale Road (1) – a clear run for Bob Graham challengers bagging the first fell of the round – but more interesting off-piste approaches run up from Millbeck and Applethwaite (2–5) and, naturally enough, from Skiddaw House itself (6).

Ascent from Gale Road 5

Via Whit Beck →*3.7km/2¼ miles* ↑*570m/1875ft* ⏱*1hr 50min*

The natural first-choice ascent

1 From the hand-gate/stile at the top of Gale Road follow the bridleway left with the wall, and then the fence, to go through a second hand-gate. Here keep north beside the fence, passing the Skiddaw shepherds' **memorial**. Ahead the rebuilt trail rises above a dip, with the conifer-decorated **Whit Beck** ravine to its right. After an initial great sweep reach a gate beside a platform,

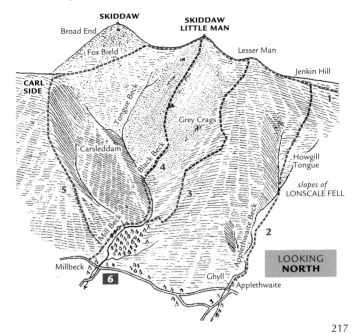

former site of a refreshment hut. Go through the gate and continue with the steady zig-zags. As you reach the brow slant northwest to reach the ridge-top fence. Do not go through the stile/hand-gate. Instead turn left and ascend the winding trail onto **Lesser Man**, with its tangle of rusting metal fence posts. Follow the ridge path rolling on northwest to the main summit.

Ascent from Millbeck 6

Brace yourself for a spot of rigorous climbing with the next three routes.

Via Howgill Tongue →3.5km/2¼ miles
↑735m/2415ft ⏱2hr 10min

A special route for lovers of heather – handfuls and ankle-twisting legfuls!

2 From the village hall walk about a kilometre down the road to **Applethwaite**, keeping on to the point where a footpath leads off from a gate, opposite a dark-green-toned cottage row. From here a woodland stroll leads to a gate and on into sunlight. The path sweeps through the swathes of bracken by a copse to reach a bench dedicated to Peter and Janie Whitaker. Ignore the path that fords the beck and sweeps left on the far bank through the gorse. Instead, gathering your energies, follow on with a path which keeps up above the **Applethwaite Gill** ravine towards a fence-stile. Beyond the fence the way steepens as you come ever closer to the gill. As you near

Heather at the top of Howgill Tongue

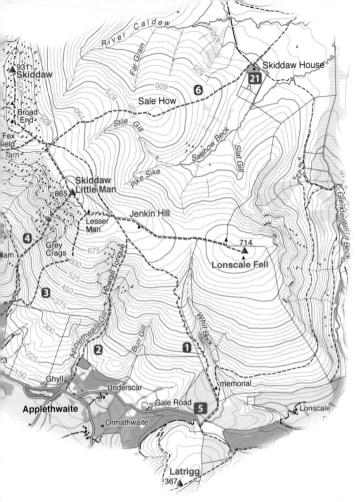

the confluence of two gills the path disappears and progress is awkward. Step across the gills onto **Howgill Tongue** and make your way up the middle of the little ridge through the heather. After a while a path emerges. Pace yourself. Eventually a small outcrop signals the last of the heather, and grass, glorious grass, leads onto the ridge. Turn left here with Route **1** on a solid highway to the summit.

Via Grey Crags
→2.5km/1½ miles
↑730m/2395ft
⏱2hr 45min

If you're looking for a workout, this is the way for you.

Weir in Mill Beck

3 Follow the drive towards the cattle grid of Ben-y-Craig and go through the hand-gate immediately left. This leads up a tight passage to a further hand-gate onto the open fell. Ignore the inviting path sweeping up left and keep to the less commonly followed grass trail leading into the valley. After a stile/locked gate the path fords Doups Gill and leads on by a silted weir, from which spills a lovely waterfall.

Ford **Mill Beck** and climb the bank directly. Bracken is an issue. There is some open ground initially but it then becomes consumed. When you reach the heather things improve. Stick to the line shown on the map and you will find broken grassy patches which allow solid progress up the fellside. After leaving the heather continue freely up by the edge of **Grey Crags** to the summit, admiring Little Man's scarred southwest slope as you go. At **Lesser Man** join the ridge path northwest for a short distance to bag your summit.

Via the southwest arête →2.4km/1½ miles ↑735m/2400ft ⏱3hr

You'll feel chuffed you took this route on. Dig deep as every stumble and grasp confirms your pioneering spirit.

4 Follow Route **3** as far as the weir. Here, instead of dipping down to the ford, stay with the path heading north to traverse well above the west side of **Mill Beck**, coming over several exciting ledges. Pass a solitary larch tree and leave the path, fording **Slades Beck** to follow up the left-hand (north) side of **Black Beck**, every inch a minor gill. There is no path. Keep with the gill until you reach a rash of scree, then trend leftwards to find the first hints of a rocky rib and reach a shelf. From here onwards follow the rocky spine of the southwest arête – pure fun and no cause for haste – all the way to the summit.

Via Carl Side →3.8km/2½ miles ↑805m/2640ft ⏱2hr 45min

An inventive route which includes a novel slanting traverse of Broad End via Fox Bield

5 Set out with Route **3** but not for long. Take the early path sweeping up left on a carpet of grass. Shortly tackle a fence-stile and reach a broken wall. Continue, passing the quartz outcrop of White Stones, now on a well-engineered path. This comes over the summit of **Carl Side** and into Carlside Col. Bend half-right by a cairn and slant at an easy angle across the slopes of **Broad End**. A path persists across the fine scree and rises to and just above the quartz outcrop of **Fox Bield**. Keep a little up from the outcrop and quickly step onto grass once more, drawing over to join the regular path. Descend to where a branch-path forks right, above the fence gate, and follow this down by the fence to pass through the depression and up onto the summit.

Ascent from Skiddaw House 21

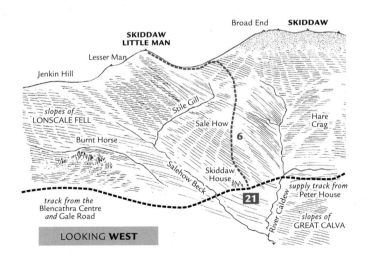

LOOKING **WEST**

Via Sale How →*3.4km/2 miles* ↑*430m/1415ft* ⏱*1hr 40min*

The first part of a neat anti-clockwise round with Lonscale Fell from the hostel

6 From the access gate to the hostel enclosure turn up left, heading southwest from the bedraggled copse onto the damp heather-decked ridge and crossing **Sale How**. The path dips through a shallow damp patch before completing a grassy climb to the hand-gate/stile in the fence that runs under the eastern scree slopes of Skiddaw. Go through the gate and left with the fence to run through the depression with Route **5** to the summit.

The summit

A small understated cairn is the sideshow to a thrilling panorama. From here the fells surrounding the Caldew basin are seen in better proportion than from big brother Skiddaw. But all eyes will be fixed on the fells surrounding and beyond Derwentwater in the southern arc. Stroll down the south slope to sit beside the bristling rocks and soak up the view.

Safe descent

Head SE down over Lesser Man to meet the popular path (**1**) at the fence and follow this trail SE down to Gale Road for Keswick. The SW slopes are no place for man or goat.

Looking down on Carsleddam

Looking back from the Skiddaw ridge path on Broad End

Ridge routes

Lonscale Fell →2.2km/1½ miles ↓195m/640ft ↑50m/165ft ⏱45min
Descend SE via the metal-tangled cairn on Lesser Man, continuing downhill to the regular thoroughfare. Cross straight over and keep company with the ridge fence to pass the cairn on Jenkin Hill. At the next depression go through the hand-gate and, now with the fence on your right, rise to a hurdle-gate and soon step onto the open summit.

Skiddaw →1.6km/1 mile ↓60m/195ft ↑125m/410ft ⏱35min
Head NW following the fence up, and where this turns right continue on to join forces with the popular path climbing to the south top. Go right, along the open ridge, to reach the OS column.

223

28 SOUTHER FELL 522M/1713FT

Climb it from	Mousthwaite Comb **1** or Mungrisdale **36**
Character	Flat-topped ridge connecting to the mighty Blencathra at Mousthwaite Col
Fell-friendly route	3
Summit grid ref	NY 354 291
Link it with	Blencathra
Part of	The Blencathra Round

Viewed from northeastern approaches, the rising ridge of Souther (traditionally pronounced 'sooter') Fell has all the appearance of a cobbler's last, which is apt as the fell name, originally Suterfell Mount, means 'cobbler's hill pasture'. Encircled by the lovely River Glenderamackin, running north and then south on its course to the River Greta and the Irish Sea, the fell is the southeastern cornerstone of the range. As such it is often the tailpiece to a high fell-round over Blencathra from Mungrisdale.

Souther Fell is the site of a ghost story from the time of the Jacobite Rebellion, when fear of marching armies was rife. The so-called Spectral Army was seen marching along the skyline in 1735, ten years before Bonnie Prince Charlie's abortive campaign. Local farm labourer Mr Lancaster witnessed it and, from his first report, the story grew and grew as more authoritative and respected figures sought to explain the curious tale.

↑ *Souther Fell's eastern aspect rising above the River Glenderamackin*

As the fell is a simple ridge, approaches conform to the basic top-to-toe orientation, with the exception of a old shepherds' drove up the eastern flank (3).

Ascent from Mousthwaite Comb 1

Via Mousthwaite Comb →*2.6km/1½ miles* ↑*295m/970ft* ⏱*1hr 10min*

Mousthwaite provides a really pleasing start to expeditions onto the ridge.

SOUTHER FELL

LOOKING **NORTH**

5

Mousthwaite
Col

Mousthwaite
Comb

slopes of
SCALES FELL

1

1

2

> road from
Scales

Path climbing out of Mousthwaite Comb

1 Walk back up the rise to a footpath sign 'Blackhazel Beck' which leads to a kissing-gate. This popular path runs on up **Mousthwaite Comb** and curves to the shallow saddle, often referred to as **Mousthwaite Col**, for all its modest elevation. From the broad saddle a clear ridge path mounts the grassy slope east and rises onto the undulating ridge-top. Part-way along the ridge detour a little left to visit a viewpoint cairn before reverting to the main ridge path to reach the cairnless summit.

Via the south ridge →*3.2km/2 miles* ↑*305m/1000ft* ⏱*1hr 40min*

Mousthwaite Col can also be reached by means of a delightful grassy shepherds' trod from a little further along the by-road.

2 Walk along the road for less than half a kilometre to find a green-way leading up from a gate. This heads west to pass below a small

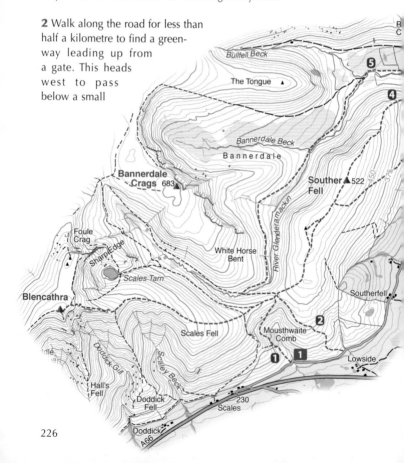

outcrop shrouded in gorse and then curves up to slant left and round a shoulder directly overlooking Mousthwaite Comb. Above the bracken-line the way contours to **Mousthwaite Col** in the form of a pronounced sheep trod. From here follow Route **1** to the summit.

Ascent from Mungrisdale 36

Across the eastern slopes →2.4km/1½ miles ↑300m/985ft ⏱1hr 10min

Another route following in the footsteps of shepherds

3 From the Mill Inn follow the gated by-road south towards Scales. Step off right immediately after the road-gate, but continue south beside the road until a shoulder shortly invites you to rise and swing right to ford a tiny gill. From this point the drove-way becomes more pronounced and leads steadily across the bracken-clothed eastern flank of the fell unhindered. The way pounds on above the bracken to swing right onto the ridge-top path in the shallow depression, some 250 metres south of the summit.

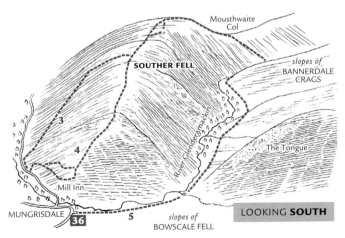

Via the north ridge →2.3km/1½ miles ↑300m/985ft ⏱1hr

The best and most direct way to the top

4 Step out with Route **3** as far as the first road-gate. After going through this step up right. Walk up with the field-bounding fence-bank on your right. As you bend right with the bank you have a choice. The first option is to follow the fence-bank and cross a gill before rising up through the bracken to a way-mark post and then heading back left up the ridge. The second option is to slant almost at once up the bracken bank and curve through a gill re-entrant to gain the ridge between two rocky steps. Both routes then unite to clamber up and enjoy a simple pleasant ridge ascent. The bracken is soon lost as you stride easily on to claim the ultimate ground.

Via the Glenderamackin valley →5.8km/3½ miles ↑325m/1065ft ⏱2hr 10min

A wander within a sequestered glen before you sweep over the felltop – a perfect combination (but best saved for a dry spell)

5 Cross the footbridge opposite the community hall and pass the Mill Inn, swinging round to the right with the by-road. After crossing the bridge bear up left to the sharp bend. Here go left along the short lane, passing on by Bannerdale View to enter the dale at a gate. Follow on with the open track, which crosses the **Bullfell Beck** footbridge and promptly steps left with the riverside path. The path, which is prone to flooding, fords **Bannerdale Beck**, with its little waterfall. Drying out a little, the green trail brushes on through the bracken. The natural curve of the valley swings under **White Horse Bent**; watch for the path angling left down to the plank footbridge. Take this to cross the bridge and switch back up to the broad saddle of **Mousthwaite Col** to join the ridge path left. Hold to its sure line which rises onto the ridge-top and leads on towards the summit with Route **1**.

Winter sunrise over Blencathra and Bannerdale Crags (photo: Mike Rowbottom)

The summit

A long, gently undulating, grassy ridge dotted with mossy pools comes briefly to a dry, rocky high point. Blink and you'll miss it – there is no cairn. The most gloriest view is westwards to Bannerdale Crags and, peering over its left shoulder, the stirring saddleback of Blencathra.

Safe descents

In poor weather refrain from leaving the summit W, as the slope is rough and in parts breaks into crags. The ridge path is a sure guide N to Mungrisdale (**4**) or S to Scales via Mousthwaite Col and Comb (**1**).

Ridge route

Blencathra →*4.2km/2½ miles* ↓*100m/330ft* ↑*440m/1445ft* ⊕*2hr*
Follow the clear ridge path SW for 1.6km (1 mile) then continue as the path swings SW into the grassy saddle of Mousthwaite Col. Continue ahead up the facing fellside on a constant path to gain the crest of Scales Fell. Curve round the rim, soon finding evidence of Fix the Fells' engineering as the trail winds on above Doddick Fell top to gain the rim of Saddleback's summit plateau. The summit lies a short distance left.

29 ULLOCK PIKE 690M/2264FT

Climb it from	High Side **19**, Rabbit Warren **18** or Old Sawmill Tearoom **17**
Character	Great rising edge of heather high above Bassenthwaite, a rousing prelude to Skiddaw itself
Fell-friendly route	1
Summit grid ref	NY 244 288
Link it with	Long Side
Part of	The Skiddaw Skyline

Ullock Pike is the striking northwestern high point of chiselled Longside Edge, much admired from the north. Sitting on a ridge which forms the western wall of Southerndale and leads up to the pass between Carl Side and Broad End, it is also a natural stopping point en route to Skiddaw. Those who do linger will not be disappointed by the panorama, swinging round from the Solway in the north to the Eastern Fells, Helvellyn among them, to the south.

Less than two kilometres west of the summit, on the shores of Bassenthwaite, sits the little church of St Bega. Dating from about AD950, it is dedicated to a Celtic saint who also gave her name to St Bees on the west coast of Cumbria, where she alighted, from Ireland, in the 9th century. A 36-mile long-distance

↑ *Ullock Pike's southern aspect from above Barf*

path, St Bega's Way, links the two places, and has more recently provided the route for a single-day ultramarathon.

Routes to the top are limited to the Edge (1–2) and an adventurous clamber up above Longside Plantation by way of the Hanging Stone (3).

Ascent from High Side 19

Via Watches →*3.2km/2 miles* ↑*520m/1710ft* ⏱*1hr 45min*

The most elegant line sweeps up the narrow ridge from the north.

1 From the layby go through the gate/stile and bear half-left with the track, rising beside the gorse. Where this ends turn right beside the old hedge-line, and when this runs out switch up left to follow the trace of a track to a gate and then cross a field to a gate/ladder-stile. This green track comes over the ridge pasture and swings right above **Southerndale Beck**. Step off the track right and follow the green path as it slants up to **Watches**, a fascinating assemblage of igneous rocks. The ridge path switches delightfully through the heather to climb **the Edge**. Only in its

later stages does the ridge encounter rock obstacles, all easily avoided or negotiated. A false top is quickly followed by the summit peak.

The Edge rising to the perfect ridge-end peak of the summit, from the Watches

Ascent from Rabbit Warren 18

Via the Edge →2.8km/1¾ miles ↑550m/1800ft ⊕1hr 30min

A sneaky sideways approach to the Edge

2 From the car park go right and quickly meet up with a path leading left (northeast). Follow this, with felled plantation to the left, and come up to a hand-gate, where a more direct footpath from the Ravenstone Hotel comes in. Head up with the fence on your left and shortly take a footpath which breaks up right to gain the heather-decked ridge. Turn right, joining Route **1**.

Ascent from Old Sawmill Tearoom 17

Via Longside Wood →3km/2 miles ↑555m/1820ft ⊕2hr 20min

The more adventurous option

3 Above the café cross the footbridge to join the tarmac roadway rising on the north side of **Skill Beck** amid mature conifers. Persist with the unenclosed roadway, and shortly after a felled area switch left with a lateral green track which rises to join a more substantial forest track. Keep left for 200 metres and then branch right and rise with the little-trodden track through the conifers.

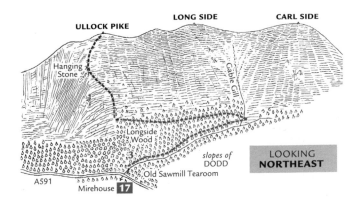

233

When the track hairpins back right into an old shepherds' path, continue straight on over rough pathless ground a matter of 50 metres to a stile in the forest-bounding fence. Here turn up right with the fence. As this corners right

The Hanging Stone

head up the rank-heather slope, holding a left bias, to reach the edge of the Hanging Stone, a small pulpit rock with a fine view of Bassenthwaite Lake. Keep on up the fellside's tough, pathless heather slope to reach the summit.

The summit

The summit provides a view to match expectations. Long Side and the grey slate-streaked bulk of Skiddaw across Southerndale captivate. Yet your attention will turn to enjoy the bird's-eye view of Bassenthwaite, with the coastal plain beyond, and then all the excitement of fells crowding in the southern arc above Dodd. Preeminent in the vista, which begins in the east with Helvellyn and runs round by Derwentwater, backed by the Scafells, is the Northwestern group, rising above Rough Mire, the wide marshy head of Bassenthwaite Lake.

Safe descents

Stay with the regular ridge path N, with all the caution confined to the early steps, bound for High Side (**1**) or Ravenstone (**2**).

Ridge route

Long Side →*0.5km/¼ mile* ↓*5m/15ft* ↑*60m/195ft* ⏱*10min*
The ridge path SE does all the talking – all you have to do is the walking!

30 WHINLATTER 517M/1696FT

Climb it from	Whinlatter Pass **7**, Hobcarton **8** or Spout Force **9**
Character	Rough heathery fell projecting from the forestry and little troubled by crowds
Fell-friendly route	4
Summit grid ref	NY 191 251
Link it with	Lord's Seat
Part of	The Aiken Beck Horseshoe

The southernmost peak of the little group that forms the Lord's Seat massif, Whinlatter must be considered the true guardian of Whinlatter Pass, and is seen clearly, soaring above the twisting road, by travellers from Lorton. Viewed from higher up the Whinlatter Pass, the long scree-streaked slopes look uninviting, but there are easier ways to reach the top, and when you do the views are superb.

Strangely, the highest point on this section of the fell, known as Whinlatter Top (526m/1726ft), has, by fellwalking convention, been relegated to subsidiary status, while Brown How (517m/1696ft) is the acknowledged summit.

Routes to the top are limited by forest-bounding fences and, of course, the steepness of the southern declivity. Nonetheless, circuits can be deftly crafted using four high keyholes and tracks in the valleys of both Whinlatter Gill (1–2) and Aiken Beck (3–4).

↑ *Whinlatter (Brown How) from the Blaze Beck valley*

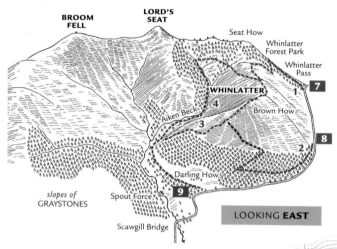

Ascent from Whinlatter Pass 7

Via Whinlatter Top → *2.8km/1¾ miles*
↑*245m/805ft* ⊕*1hr 10min*

Switchback through the forest park to the ridge.

1 Walk out of the car park and down to the roadside layby at the forest edge, to the west of the park entrance. Pass the barrier and ascend the green track. Ignore the first green path left and rise, passing beneath the red-squirrel ropeway, to reach the large sweeping bend, with its squirrel-habitat panel. Here turn left, off the main track, following the forest track due west. Rise easily to a turning bay and, beyond this, a hand-gate in the forest-boundary fence. Go through, turn abruptly uphill, beside the fence, and climb steeply to arrive

quickly on the ridge-top. Resume your westward course, coming over the true summit. Duly slip through the cross-ridge wall, advancing into heather and to the west top, **Brown How**, with its curved shelter.

Ascent from Hobcarton 8

Via western slopes →2.4km/1½ miles ↑270m/885ft ⊕1hr 20min

A more adventurous way up the western slopes

2 Step back onto the road and go left, looking for the gateway and barrier on the right. Here embark on a forest track which largely contours at first. This rises and at its highest point reaches a ramped green-way which switches acutely back right within the forestry. Take this old drove as it leads through a wall-gateway in the dark of the forest and comes up to

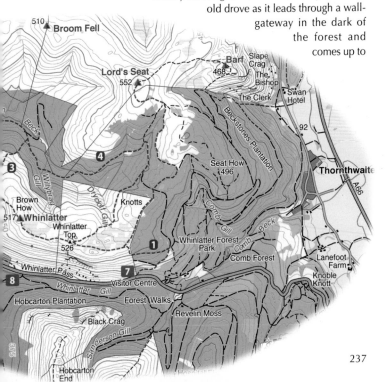

a partial clearing. At this point find a plain fence in the broken wall bounding the maturing plantation. Cross this and bear half-left, with hints of sheep trods and the odd fellwanderers' path giving encouragement, and avoid the scree and minor outcropping. Aim for the skyline on the same trajectory. A strong sheep path leads steadily back along the edge to the summit, becoming more certain as you travel.

Ascent from Spout Force 9

These two routes combine beautifully to make a tidy circuit, best followed anti-clockwise.

Via Aiken Beck valley →*2.8km/1¾ miles* ↑*280m/920ft* ⏱*1hr*
3 Follow the forest track, passing the barrier at **Darling How Farm**, ignoring the first track drifting left into the valley and then ignoring the next track which switches acutely right. Keep on for a further 200 metres to find a cluster of small rocks set in the form of an arrow on the right. Clamber up

Aiken Beck valley track

the eroded bank and weave a course up through the conifers beside a wall to an awkward fence-corner with a shoddy substitute for a stile (you may opt to cross a little above). Keep up beside the fence and, as this turns right, find a continuing path mounting the heathery fell to the stone wind-break on **Brown How**.

Via Whinlatter Top →4.8km/3 miles ↑300m/985ft ⏱2hr

4 Start out as for Route **3** but keep on with the forest track, past all the paths leading off, up the **Aiken Beck** valley. As you get towards the head of the valley and cross the beck for a final time, this track switches south and climbs more steeply into the young forest. Watch for a minor, level, cleared trackway branching half-right, which leads through to a stile in the bounding fence, where a fence converges on the far side. A regular path ensues, contouring to ford **Drycloff Gill** before wandering upwards over the rough moor-grass terrain to unite with the main ridge path on **Whinlatter Top**, the true summit. From here follow the ridge to reach **Brown How**, the acknowledged summit.

The summit

Whinlatter Top, with its more conventional cairn, is a proper summit right enough. Yet it is the west top that is the better viewing station, and in my book situation and setting are significant factors in identifying a summit. The Hobcarton Gill valley, focused on Ladyside Pike and Hopegill Head, and, nearer left, Hobcarton End, backed by Grisedale Pike, are strong subjects for any camera, and the turf is a fine place to sit and contemplate the larks in the sky. If you

High-perched sheepfold on the southern flank of Brown How

fancy a spot of exploration you might be tempted to pay a visit to an unusually sited but well-preserved sheepfold set on a tiny shelf some 100 metres down the heather bank, SSE of Brown How and unseen from the ridge path.

Safe descents

Any route S would be a bad move. Head E along the ridge, turning down right at the point where the forest fence is met to find a hand-gate and the security of a forest track for Whinlatter Pass (**1**). If you follow the same fence NE you can exit the moor at a hand-gate; the ensuing path leads through a tunnel of trees to the forest track, where you can turn left and comfortably wander down to Spout Force.

Ridge route

Lord's Seat →*3.6km/2¼ miles* ↓*55m/180ft* ↑*90m/295ft* ⏱*1hr 15min*
Follow the ridge E, coming to the bounding fence. Bend left, dipping to come close to the fence and continuing to a hand-gate in the northeast corner of the open fell enclosure. The path slips through a tunnel, crossing a section of the Altura bikers' trail. The path emerges onto a fully fledged forest track at an enlarged sweeping junction. Turn right, heading NE, and keep left at the next junction (avoiding the Altura route straight on). The forest track becomes almost level and dwindles to a path, which advances through cross-paths to climb to the prominent summit beyond the forest fence.

Bield on Brown How

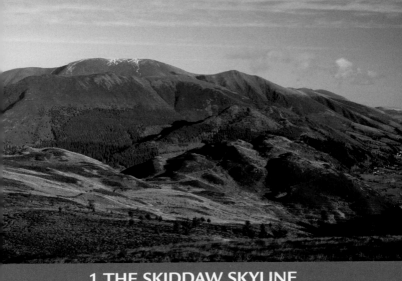

1 THE SKIDDAW SKYLINE

Start/Finish	Bassenthwaite (or High Side **19** or Peter House Farm **20**)
Distance	14.5km (9 miles)
Ascent/Descent	940m (3085ft)
Time	7hr
Terrain	A steep ascent by the fence onto Bakestall, followed by a steady plod over Skiddaw; descent to Carl Side, avoiding the worst of the ubiquitous slate scree; only minor rock-steps on the lovely ridge down by Ullock Pike
Summits	Bakestall, Skiddaw, Carl Side, Long Side and Ullock Pike

A fine horseshoe expedition, starting with dramatic views of Dash Falls and Dead Crags and culminating on Skiddaw, with pastoral beauty to begin with and a simple high-level traverse which enjoys the best qualities of a fine mountain, especially the final flourish – Longside Edge.

Start from the bus stop at the northern corner of the tree-lined green in Bassenthwaite village. Go right by Back Hill and swing left by Green View. The cul-de-sac leads through a concreted stock passage to reach a field-gate. Bear left, following the young hawthorn hedge, then the fence, to a gate and

↑ Skiddaw massif from Lord's Seat

go straight across the next field to a stile/gate in a fence. From here angle half-right to a hand-gate in the field corner. Accompany the tree-bowered fence to a stile, then on to a hand-gate, and beyond to reach a bridle-crossways. Here, in step with the Cumbria Way, follow the sign to **Peter House** ahead. Pass through the passage by the boulder to a stile/field-gate. Advance onto the open track, passing to the right of the farm buildings, to a gate onto the Orthwaite road (**20**).

Cross straight over by the gate to follow the gated open road leading handsomely up the Dash valley. Where a track forks right, follow suit to reach and cross the plank-bridge over Dead Beck and go through a gate. Swing up under the combe to reach the top of **Whitewater Dash** (Dash Falls) and a gate. Don't go through. Instead keep to the west side of the rising wall (which soon becomes a fence) on a steady ascent up **Birkett Edge**. Plod patiently up to the brow, where the fence turns beside a cairn and a ridge-top path can be followed right to visit the summit cairn of **Bakestall**.

Approaching Whitewater Dash along the Skiddaw House track

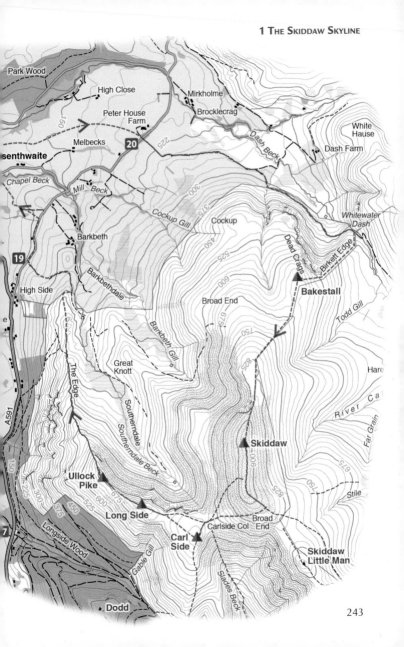

Park Wood

High Close

Mirkholme

Brocklecrag

Peter House
Farm

White
Hause

Dash Farm

Melbecks

20

senthwaite

Chapel Beck

Mill Beck

Cockup Gill

Cockup

Whitewater
Dash

Barkbeth

19

Dead Crags

Birkett Edge

Bakestall

Barkbethdale

High Side

Broad End

Todd Gill

e

Barkbeth Gill

Hare

Great
Knott

The Edge

River Ca

Southerndale

Southerndale Beck

Skiddaw

Fat Grain

Ullock
Pike

Stile

Long Side

Carlside Col

Broad
End

A591

Carl
Side

Skiddaw
Little Man

7

Longside Wood

Gable Gill

Dodd

Slades Beck

Skiddaw Little Man from Carlside Col

Follow the fence as it passes a remnant fold and rises up the otherwise simple ridge. The slope eases as the fence again turns. Keep straight forward as the fence begins to contour away, following the ridge, climbing the inviting tapering crest to reach the lofty summit ridge of **Skiddaw**, with its modest cairn. March boldly on to the decrepit OS column marking the actual summit. The view is compelling but the really top-notch view is yet to come. The cairned ridge dips and rises. Press on to the cairn on **Broad End** south top for a stupendous view over the Lake District fells.

Follow the regular path southeast, descending towards the depression before Little Man. However, comfortably above the dip, take your own initiative and angle right, finding comparatively easy ground with some grass and flaky slate, wary to keep above Fox Bield to avoid stumbling on chunky slate. Lower down you might find the trace of a casual path as you soon merge with the more direct descent from Broad End. Come down to **Carlside Col** with its pools.

Strike on to the cairn on the crown of **Carl Side** with its sumptuous perspective on Skiddaw Little Man and a view down onto Carsleddam, consumed in dense heather. **Long Side** is a further delight, lacking only a decent summit cairn. Follow **the Edge** in pleasing stepped stages, with rank heather on the Bassenthwaite slope and the deep hollow of Southerndale to the right.

The summit of **Ullock Pike** makes a wonderful vantage from which to view the lower stages of the ridge. Apart from an easily evaded little rock-step, it is a comfortable walk.

The ridge path draws down to a wall (ignore the inviting hand-gate). Follow this right to meet a track and go left by the stile/gate, now on a green track, down a pasture, curving left. Go through successive gates, keeping with the track to bend down right to a gate onto the Orthwaite road once more (**19**). Go right, passing High Side House. Keep an eye out for a stile and footpath sign left. Step over the ditch and aim half-right to a stile in the field boundary below an ageing oak beside a solitary stone gatepost. Turn left and follow the track but don't go through the gate. Keep the fence to your left as far as a hedge. Here go right via a stile and, as the hedge corners, go left down to another stile. At the foot of the next field cross a further stile and come alongside **Chapel Beck**. After another gate cross the footbridge and then, in the field corner, a final stone stile in the hedge, stepping onto the road. Follow this back to **Bassenthwaite** village green.

Looking back to Ullock Pike from Watches

2 THE BLENCATHRA ROUND

Start/Finish	Mungrisdale **36**
Distance	14.5km (9 miles)
Ascent/Descent	890m (2920ft)
Time	6hr
Terrain	Open heath and pasture until the head of the Glenderamackin; steeper ground and a loose trail to Atkinson Pike; good paths thereafter until the tail end of Souther Fell, which is consumed in dense bracken
Summits	Bowscale Fell, Bannerdale Crags, Blencathra and Souther Fell

A wonderfully rewarding skyline walk which sets its ambition on striding across the great saddle of Blencathra, while also capturing three fine fells around the headwaters of the Glenderamackin.

Walk up the path and stone steps round to the right of the village hall to a wicket-gate, and follow the fence to a metal gate back onto the road. Carry on past St Kentigern's church and round a right-hand bend to a junction, where

↑ *Walkers following the ridge path to Bannerdale Crags,*
with imposing Blencathra beyond

The distinctive 'saddleback' profile of Blencathra from across the head of Bannerdale

the road begins to rise. Just past this turn left onto the short lane behind the dwellings to a rickety wooden gate. From here bear up right, above the old quarry and through the gorse thicket – much easier to ascend than descend! Duly the slope eases as the path comes onto pasture then reaches the edge of the heather moor, making up the broad ridge. Pass cairns at each crest of the rising ridge as you make your way above Bowscale Tarn. Make sure you take the time to step off the path to peer down and admire this perfect glacial corrie. The ridge angles half-left to pass a cairn and, a little further, the wind-break on the actual summit of **Bowscale Fell**, at the apex of the Tongue.

View from the summit of Blencathra west to Gategill Fell top, with Skiddaw to the right

Follow on south, choosing the path that angles left to hug the head-wall rim of **Bannerdale**, and rise to the cairn at the top of the east ridge of **Bannerdale Crags**. Walk due west down to the col at the source of the **River Glenderamackin**. Here turn up southwest on the steeply rising path, which takes three steps to reach the northern top above **Foule Crag**. The long saddle traverse features two quartz crosses and a wind-whipped pool short of the final tilt to the summit of **Blencathra** (Hall's Fell top). It's all about the view!

From here take flight east down the zig-zag path. Swing above the awesomely deep **Scaley Beck** valley, its slopes richly clothed in heather in season, onto the narrow rim of **Scales Fell**. Watch for the first path fork. Here go left down the grassy pasture slope onto the long saddle of Mousthwaite Col. Two paths cross south to north. Strike straight through and up the facing path onto **Souther Fell**.

This path curves north along the pasture top through some peaty patches. Make a point of visiting the obvious cairn to gaze at Bannerdale Crags, but note that Souther Fell itself has no cairn at the summit. The ridge path descends and comes into bracken. After a brief rock-step take the more direct of two available lines. Reach the intake wall and follow it south until the fence-bank ends and a quick step down brings you to the tarmac road at a gate. Go through to complete the walk, passing the Mill Inn and a footbridge to return to the start point.

Souther Fell from a very wintry Mousthwaite Col

3 THE NORTHERN CROWN

Start/Finish	Mosedale **33**
Distance	20km (12½ miles)
Ascent/Descent	866m (2840ft)
Time	6½ hr
Terrain	Easy going to the Lingy Hut but then marshy ground onto Knott and briefly on the initial ridge of Great Calva; an ankle-twisting descent trail in the heather, leading to a firm track and roadway
Summits	Carrock Fell, High Pike, Knott and Great Calva

Prime fellwalking territory, sweeping over four quite distinct fells that together form the northernmost headland of the Lake District – Carrock Fell, High Pike, Knott and Great Calva – mingling heather and grassland, concluding with the excited waters of the Caldew.

Follow the road leading west through the hamlet into the Caldew valley. Passing the Town End sign, as the bracken ceases drift onto a path beside a grassy patch. When you reach a small prostrate juniper switch right and angle up the slope of low bracken and heather. Here the path kinks left and continues

↑ *Interlocking ridges above the Caldew valley, from the ridge above Bowscale Tarn*

through light scree and heather until forced to hold to the top of scree by a barrier of gorse coming over a tiny rock-step. Turn left to arrive immediately at a crescent-shaped bield. The path climbs on, passing a larger bield-wall, and brushes through the rampant heather. (Only one

Looking back at Carrock Fell from Miton Hill

bield is marked on the OS map but it doesn't match up with either of these!) The path completes its ascent of **Carrock Fell** at a large ruined fold, built of stone from the ringwork that casts an elongated necklace of pinkish boulders around the tilted summit area. Bear left to the summit cairn.

The ridge path heads on west over much damp ground. Round Knott may draw you off the normal path but is well moated. Once you reach dry grass the way flows effortlessly as you dip to cross the faint Red Gate path and then rise and swing right above the scoured banks of **Drygill Beck**. Cross a cart-track to complete the northward ascent of **High Pike**. A stout slate bench, an unusual piece of summit furniture, stands before the ragged wind-break cairn. A further (nettle-filled) wind-break sits a little way down the northern slope.

Blencathra from the summit of Great Calva

Retrace your ascent to the cart-track and then follow this south over **Hare Stones** in harmony with the Cumbria Way to pass the Lingy Hut bothy. Although the track leading down to the crossing of the **Miller Moss** basin is marshy, firmer ground is found on the facing rise onto **Coomb Height**. Swing right (west) along the ridge to reach the crest of **Knott**, where a small cairn admirably performs its duty on the bare grassy dome.

From here take the southwesterly path down to the hause at the source of **Wiley Gill**.

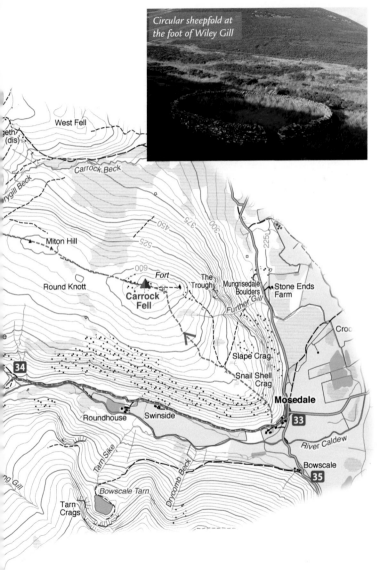

Circular sheepfold at the foot of Wiley Gill

West Fell

Carrock Beck

geth (dis)

rygill Beck

Miton Hill

Round Knott

600

Fort

Carrock
Fell

The Trough

Mungrisedale
Boulders

Further Gill

Stone Ends
Farm

450

375

525

300

225

Croo

Slape Crag

Snail Shell
Crag

Mosedale

34

Roundhouse   Swinside

33

River Caldew

Tarn Sike

Dorycomb Beck

Bowscale

35

g Gill

Bowscale Tarn

Tarn
Crags

The path is strong as it slants leftward onto the damp moor. A stile in the ridge fence sits amid a pool. Cross the metal hurdle to its left and switch sides smartly to climb **Great Calva** on a southeasterly course. The summit cairn is supported by a wind-break over the fence, ready to shield pausing walkers from prevailing winds. Follow the fence to the slightly lower fence-corner top for the better view.

The next phase of the walk – the final descent – is uncomfortable, a steep stumbling way through unforgivingly dense heather. The thin path is best ignored when wet as it's slippery. Keep to the cushion of heather to ease your feet. At long long last the slope eases and you reach a lateral path leading right. Even this has a tricky ending as it funnels through a water-worn gully to reach the bank of **Wiley Gill** and so join the main valley track beside the handsome circular sheepfold.

Cross the wooden footbridge and pass through the hand-gate. The track is your sure guide down the glen, following the **River Caldew** – a considerable watercourse. Cross the **Grainsgill Beck** bridge. The track becomes a road for the final 20 minutes of the walk back to Mosedale and your starting point.

Blencathra and Great Calva

4 THE AIKEN BECK HORSESHOE

Start/Finsh	Spout Force **9**
Distance	13km (8 miles)
Ascent/Descent	610m (2000ft)
Time	5hr
Terrain	Comfortable forest tracks lead to a stiff pull onto the crown of Graystones, followed by open pasture to Lord's Seat; more forest tracks ensue to the marshy top of Whinlatter and beyond, including one awkward fence-crossing after Brown How.
Summits	Graystones, Broom Fell, Lord's Seat and Whinlatter

Keep above the conifer canopy of Whinlatter to claim the four notable tops that make up the Lord's Seat massif: Graystones, Broom Fell, Lord's Seat itself and Whinlatter – a liberating short trip.

From the parking area follow the open forestry track, passing the barrier close to **Darling How** farm. As the track gently descends take care to bear left with the forest track (junction post 28) which then bears right as it crosses **Aiken Beck** bridge. Shortly the track switches back left. At the next fork (junction post 29) go left and then, after crossing a gill, bear up right on a rougher

↑ *Broom Fell and Lord's Seat from Graystones*

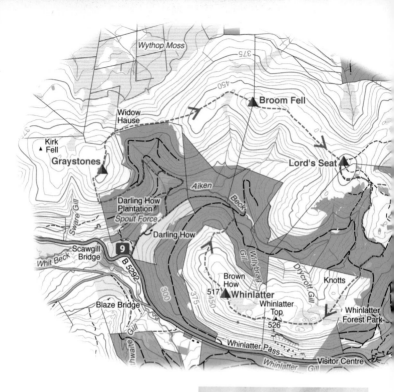

forest track. This arrives at a track intersection, where the slope ahead was newly felled in 2019. Swing left on the forest track and, where this track hairpins right (junction post 30), keep forward on a confined path, heather lined and somewhat hemmed in by conifers, which opens onto a cut shelf leading to the forest-bounding fence and broken wall. Step over and climb the comparatively short slope beside the broken wall.

Wall overlooking a rock-step below the summit of Graystones

View back to Broom Fell from Lord's Seat

Above the fence-corner scramble up a rock-step and keep climbing until the slopes eases. At this point bear right to reach the summit of **Graystones** (the highest of three contenders).

From here set off north-northeast over the brow, descending to the fence. At the foot of the slope clamber through the fence pen and follow on east with the ridge, coming over the knoll of **Widow Hause**. Walk unencumbered up and along the open ridge to arrive at the handsome cairn and wind-break marking the crown of **Broom Fell**.

Cross the stile and dip down again to go through a hand-gate and through a damp patch, trending southeast across Todd Fell to climb onto the top of **Lord's Seat**. The outlook is impressive, especially towards the Skiddaw massif.

Descend south to the stile in the forest-bounding fence, now on a gravel path through heather liberally sprinkled with firs. Arriving at a path-fork (junction post 5) go right. This path evolves into a forest track and winds alarmingly

Tarbarrel Moss track intersection

– enough to disorientate even the most geographically astute. After passing a fenced-off scree slope on the right, reach a substantial forest track intersection (junction post 3, Tarbarrel Moss).

The track ahead descends into the Aiken Beck valley, while that to

the left leads down to the Whinlatter Visitor Centre. Take neither of these but dive into the dense conifer canopy on a path immediately left of the signed Altura bike trail. The bike trail swings across the line of the path. Continue on to arrive at a hand-gate in the corner of the forest-bounding fence. (The small boggy hollow is Tarbarrel Moss.) The path through the heather keeps beside the left-hand forest-edge fence. When the fence dips the path forks.

Summit wind-break on Brown How

Keep beside the fence to find the spine of the ridge and turn right to reach **Whinlatter Top** with its tiny cairn. Slip through a broken cross-ridge wall to the wind-break on **Brown How**, the (customary) summit of Whinlatter.

Follow the path curving north off the ridge, dipping to a bounding wall and fence. Bear right, following the wall-side fence. This dips to a corner where you will find a shoddy substitute for a stile (you may opt to cross a little above). The path continues down, keeping intimate company with the wall and conifers, the last bank step onto the forest track a little awkward. Turn left and follow the track down back to the start.

MORE TO EXPLORE

Circular

- from Longlands **26**: Longlands Fell–Lowthwaite Fell–Brae Fell–Little Sca Fell–Great Sca Fell–Meal Fell–Great Cockup
- from Millbeck **6**: Carl Side–Skiddaw–Skiddaw Little Man–Lonscale Fell

Winter heather aglow in evening sun on the southern slopes of Ling Fell

USEFUL CONTACTS

Tourist information

The centre at the Market Hall in the centre of Keswick is the only National Park information centre in the area covered by this guide, but lots of information is available on the National Park website: www.lakedistrict.gov.uk.

Keswick
tel 0845 901 0845
(calls cost 2p per minute plus your phone company's access charge)
KeswickTIC@lake-district.gov.uk

Accommodation

In addition to the tourist information centres and search engines, the Visit Cumbria website has a good database of local accommodation options: www.visitcumbria.com.

Weather

It is well worth consulting either of these forecasts to gauge the best times to be on the tops.

Lake District Weatherline
tel 0844 846 2444
www.lakedistrictweatherline.co.uk

Mountain Weather Information Service
Full mountain forecasts for
3 days at a time
www.mwis.org.uk
(choose English and Welsh Forecast/
Lake District)
App: Mountain Forecast Viewer

Transport

Traveline
Information on buses, trains and coaches – such as they are
www.traveline.info

Stagecoach
Bus information
www.stagecoachbus.com
App: Stagecoach Bus

Organisations

The National Trust

The National Trust owns 90% of the farms in the national park, as well as historic sites and properties, camp sites and car parks.
www.nationaltrust.org.uk
App: National Trust – Days Out

Fix the Fells

Fix the Fells repairs and maintains 335 upland paths in the national park. Read about their work, volunteer or donate on this website.
www.fixthefells.co.uk

Mountain Rescue

The Lake District Search and Mountain Rescue Association manages 12 teams of volunteers across the national park. The site has useful safety information. Downloading the free OS Locate app will enable you to tell the team your grid ref, whether you have phone signal or not, should you need to call them.
www.ldsamra.org.uk

A FELLRANGER'S GLOSSARY

Navigational features

Word	Explanation
arête	knife-edge ridge
band	binding strip of land
bank-barn	barn accessible on two levels (often built on a slope or bank)
beck	main stream flowing into and through valleys to lakes and rivers
boiler-plates	non-technical term for exposed broad slabs of rock
brae	broad fell
cairn/man	small pile of loose stones indicating a path or path junction
clint	block forming part of a natural limestone pavement
combe/cove	hanging valley high in the fells
common	undivided land grazed by several farmers
cop	viewpoint
crag	substantial outcrop of rock
currick	(Cumbrian) cairn
dale	valley
dodd	rounded hilltop
drumlin	large mound that accumulated beneath a melting glacier
dub	dark pool
fell	mountain pasture, frequently attributed to the whole hill
force	waterfall
garth	small enclosure close to farm buildngs
gate	dialect term for a track
ghyll/gill	steeply sloping watercourse
glen	from British term 'glyn' meaning valley
grain	lesser watercourse above a confluence
hag	eroded section of peat moor
hause, saddle, col, dore, scarth	high gap between fells
holm	dry riverside meadow
hope	secluded valley
howe	hill or mound
ill	treacherous
intake	upper limit of valley enclosure
keld	spring
knott	compact or rugged hilltop

laithe	barn in the field or on the fell (rather than next to the farmstead)
ling	heather
lonnin	quiet lane
man	from Celtic term 'maen' meaning stone marker
mell	bald hill
mere	pool or lake
mire	marshy ground
moraine	residual valley-head pillow-mound debris left after a glacier melts away
nab, naze	hill-spur or nose
ness	promontory
nether	lower
nook	secluded corner
outcrop	crag or obvious collection of rocks
out-gang	shepherds' drove-lane to a particular fell pasture
park	enclosed hunting ground
pike	sharp or rocky summit
place	plot of ground
raise	heap of stones
rake	grooved track
ridding	(the action of) clearing
rigg	ridge
scale	summer-pasture shieling (hut)
scarp/scar	steep hillside
scree	weathered rock debris beneath a crag
seat	summer pasture/high place
shaw	small wood
sheep-creep	small field-to-field access hole/gap for sheep
shelter-cairn	circular wind-break wall
sike	small stream
slack	small, shallow or stony valley
sled-gate	track for pony-drawn sledges
slump	sedimentary rock that has slipped, creating dykes (intrusions), fractures or ridges
stang	pole
stead	site of a farm

strainer posts	posts at either end of a wire fence, between which wire is 'strained' or stretched taut
sty	steep path
swine	pigs
tarn	small mountain pool, from the Norse 'tjorn' meaning tear
thwaite	clearing
traverse	walking route across the fells
trig point	Ordnance Survey triangulation column
trod	path created by animals
wash-fold	sheepfold where sheep were once gathered for washing in the beck
water	feeder lake to a river
wath	ford
whin	gorse
wick	inlet or bay or subsidiary farm
wray	secluded corner
yeat	gate

Place names

Name	Explanation
Bewaldeth	estate associated with a woman called Aldgifu (Norse)
Brockle Crag	rocky fellside with a badger set
Brundholme	burnt meadow
Candleseaves Bog	bog from which rushes for making candles were gathered
Cocklakes	lekking (mating) ground of black grouse
Glenderamackin	glyn dwfr er mochyn (Celtic) ('river valley of the swine')
Ireby	the Irishman's farmstead
Mallen Dodd	from maoilín (Gaelic) = small rounded hillock
Mousthwaite (Comb or Col)	tiny clearing
Mungrisdale	St Mungo in the valley of swine
Orthwaite	clearing of the black cock, from orr ('black cock')
Over Water	lake of the black cock, from orr ('black cock')
Randel Crag	raven crag
Roughten (Gill)	roaring waters
Sale How	hill above the bog

Slape (Crag)	slippery rock
Trusmadoor	doorway through the great hills (Celtic)
Whinny (Brow)	gorse-filled place
White Horse Bent	from the pale colour of the grass on its slopes, 'horse' being a corruption of hause ('pass' or 'passage')
Wythop	willow (Old English)
Street Head	once thought to be at the head of a Roman road

Fell names

Just the more intriguing ones…

Name	Explanation
Bannerdale (Crags)	holly-tree valley
Barf	berg (Norse) = unassailable cliff
Binsey	possibly 'the hill with a heap'
Blencathra	dalehead seat
Bowscale Fell	the fell like the prow of a ship
Carl Side	old man's pasture (Norse)
Carrock Fell	place of the rock
Great Calva	breeding ground for deer ('calf' = fawn)
Great Cockup	high pasture lekking ground of black grouse above the blind valley
Great Sca Fell	from 'shieling' (shepherd's summer hut)
Knott	compact place
Latrigg	the fell with the lair
Lonscale Fell	quiet barn
Meal Fell	bare hill (cf moel (Welsh) and Great and Little Mell Fells)
Sale Fell	willow hill
Skiddaw	schydehow (Norse) = hill of the jutting rock (cf Scoat Fell)
Souther Fell	the cobbler's hill pasture (first recorded as Suterfell Mount)
Ullock (Pike)	hill above Ullaikmire (place name recorded near Mirehouse in 1304), 'wetland where wolf cubs play'
Whinlatter	steep gorse-covered slope

THE LAKE DISTRICT FELLS

Fell name	Height	Volume
Allen Crags	784m/2572ft	Borrowdale
Angletarn Pikes	567m/1860ft	Mardale and the Far East
Ard Crags	581m/1906ft	Buttermere
Armboth Fell	479m/1572ft	Borrowdale
Arnison Crag	434m/1424ft	Patterdale
Arthur's Pike	533m/1749ft	Mardale and the Far East
Bakestall	673m/2208ft	Keswick
Bannerdale Crags	683m/2241ft	Keswick
Barf	468m/1535ft	Keswick
Barrow	456m/1496ft	Buttermere
Base Brown	646m/2119ft	Borrowdale
Beda Fell	509m/1670ft	Mardale and the Far East
Bell Crags	558m/1831ft	Borrowdale
Binsey	447m/1467ft	Keswick
Birkhouse Moor	718m/2356ft	Patterdale
Birks	622m/2241ft	Patterdale
Black Combe	600m/1969ft	Coniston
Black Fell	323m/1060ft	Coniston
Blake Fell	573m/1880ft	Buttermere
Bleaberry Fell	589m/1932ft	Borrowdale
Blea Rigg	556m/1824ft	Langdale
Blencathra	868m/2848ft	Keswick
Bonscale Pike	529m/1736ft	Mardale and the Far East
Bowfell	903m/2963ft	Langdale
Bowscale Fell	702m/2303ft	Keswick
Brae Fell	586m/1923ft	Keswick
Brandreth	715m/2346ft	Borrowdale
Branstree	713m/2339ft	Mardale and the Far East
Brim Fell	795m/2608ft	Coniston

Fell name	Height	Volume
Brock Crags	561m/1841ft	Mardale and the Far East
Broom Fell	511m/1676ft	Keswick
Buckbarrow (Corney Fell)	549m/1801ft	Coniston
Buckbarrow (Wast Water)	430m/1411ft	Wasdale
Calf Crag	537m/1762ft	Langdale
Carl Side	746m/2448ft	Keswick
Carrock Fell	662m/2172ft	Keswick
Castle Crag	290m/951ft	Borrowdale
Catbells	451m/1480ft	Borrowdale
Catstycam	890m/2920ft	Patterdale
Caudale Moor	764m/2507ft	Mardale and the Far East
Causey Pike	637m/2090ft	Buttermere
Caw	529m/1736ft	Coniston
Caw Fell	697m/2287ft	Wasdale
Clough Head	726m/2386ft	Patterdale
Cold Pike	701m/2300ft	Langdale
Coniston Old Man	803m/2635ft	Coniston
Crag Fell	523m/1716ft	Wasdale
Crag Hill	839m/2753ft	Buttermere
Crinkle Crags	860m/2822ft	Langdale
Dale Head	753m/2470ft	Buttermere
Dodd	502m/1647ft	Keswick
Dollywaggon Pike	858m/2815ft	Patterdale
Dove Crag	792m/2599ft	Patterdale
Dow Crag	778m/2553ft	Coniston
Eagle Crag	520m/1706ft	Borrowdale
Eskdale Moor	337m/1105ft	Wasdale
Esk Pike	885m/2904ft	Langdale
Fairfield	873m/2864ft	Patterdale

Fell name	Height	Volume
Fellbarrow	416m/1365ft	Buttermere
Fleetwith Pike	648m/2126ft	Buttermere
Froswick	720m/2362ft	Mardale and the Far East
Gavel Fell	526m/1726ft	Buttermere
Gibson Knott	421m/1381ft	Langdale
Glaramara	783m/2569ft	Borrowdale
Glenridding Dodd	442m/1450ft	Patterdale
Gowbarrow Fell	481m/1578ft	Patterdale
Grange Fell	416m/1365ft	Borrowdale
Grasmoor	852m/2795ft	Buttermere
Gray Crag	697m/2287ft	Mardale and the Far East
Grayrigg Forest	494m/1621ft	Mardale and the Far East
Graystones	456m/1496ft	Keswick
Great Borne	616m/2021ft	Buttermere
Great Calva	690m/2264ft	Keswick
Great Carrs	788m/2585ft	Coniston
Great Cockup	526m/1726ft	Keswick
Great Crag	452m/1483ft	Borrowdale
Great Dodd	857m/2812ft	Patterdale
Great End	907m/2976ft	Borrowdale, Langdale, Wasdale
Great Gable	899m/2949ft	Borrowdale, Wasdale
Great How	523m/1716ft	Wasdale
Great Mell Fell	537m/1762ft	Patterdale
Great Rigg	767m/2516ft	Patterdale
Great Sca Fell	651m/2136ft	Keswick
Great Worm Crag	427m/1401ft	Coniston
Green Crag	489m/1604ft	Coniston
Green Gable	801m/2628ft	Borrowdale

Fell name	Height	Volume
Grey Crag	638m/2093ft	Mardale and the Far East
Grey Friar	772m/2533ft	Coniston
Grey Knotts	697m/2287ft	Borrowdale
Grike	488m/1601ft	Wasdale
Grisedale Pike	791m/2595ft	Buttermere
Hallin Fell	388m/1273ft	Mardale and the Far East
Hard Knott	552m/1811ft	Coniston
Harrison Stickle	736m/2415ft	Langdale
Hart Crag	822m/2697ft	Patterdale
Harter Fell (Eskdale)	653m/2142ft	Coniston
Harter Fell (Mardale)	778m/2553ft	Mardale and the Far East
Hart Side	758m/2487ft	Patterdale
Hartsop above How	586m/1923ft	Patterdale
Hartsop Dodd	618m/2028ft	Mardale and the Far East
Haycock	798m/2618ft	Wasdale
Haystacks	598m/1962ft	Buttermere
Helm Crag	405m/1329ft	Langdale
Helvellyn	950m/3116ft	Patterdale
Hen Comb	509m/1670ft	Buttermere
Heron Pike	621m/2037ft	Patterdale
Hesk Fell	476m/1562ft	Coniston
High Crag	744m/2441ft	Buttermere
High Hartsop Dodd	519m/1703ft	Patterdale
High Pike (Caldbeck)	658m/2159ft	Keswick
High Pike (Scandale Fell)	656m/2152ft	Patterdale
High Raise (Central Fells)	762m/2500ft	Langdale
High Raise (Haweswater)	802m/2631ft	Mardale and the Far East
High Rigg	355m/1165ft	Borrowdale
High Seat	608m/1995ft	Borrowdale

Fell name	Height	Volume
High Spy	653m/2142ft	Borrowdale
High Stile	807m/2648ft	Buttermere
High Street	828m/2717ft	Mardale and the Far East
High Tove	515m/1690ft	Borrowdale
Hindscarth	727m/2385ft	Buttermere
Holme Fell	317m/1040ft	Coniston
Hopegill Head	770m/2526ft	Buttermere
Ill Bell	757m/2484ft	Mardale and the Far East
Illgill Head	609m/1998ft	Wasdale
Iron Crag	640m/2100ft	Wasdale
Kentmere Pike	730m/2395ft	Mardale and the Far East
Kidsty Pike	780m/2559ft	Mardale and the Far East
Kirk Fell	802m/2631ft	Wasdale
Knock Murton	447m/1467ft	Buttermere
Knott	710m/2329ft	Keswick
Knott Rigg	556m/1824ft	Buttermere
Lank Rigg	541m/1775ft	Wasdale
Latrigg	368m/1207ft	Keswick
Ling Fell	373m/1224ft	Keswick
Lingmell	807m/2649ft	Wasdale
Lingmoor Fell	470m/1542ft	Langdale
Little Hart Crag	637m/2090ft	Patterdale
Little Mell Fell	505m/1657ft	Patterdale
Little Stand	739m/2426ft	Langdale
Loadpot Hill	671m/2201ft	Mardale and the Far East
Loft Crag	682m/2237ft	Langdale
Longlands Fell	483m/1585ft	Keswick
Long Side	734m/2408ft	Keswick
Lonscale Fell	715m/2346ft	Keswick

Fell name	Height	Volume
Lord's Seat	552m/1811ft	Keswick
Loughrigg Fell	335m/1099ft	Langdale
Low Fell	423m/1388ft	Buttermere
Low Pike	507m/1663ft	Patterdale
Maiden Moor	576m/1890ft	Borrowdale
Mardale Ill Bell	761m/2497ft	Mardale and the Far East
Meal Fell	550m/1804ft	Keswick
Mellbreak	512m/1680ft	Buttermere
Middle Dodd	653m/2143ft	Patterdale
Middle Fell	585m/1919ft	Wasdale
Muncaster Fell	231m/758ft	Coniston
Nab Scar	450m/1476ft	Patterdale
Nethermost Pike	891m/2923ft	Patterdale
Outerside	568m/1863ft	Buttermere
Pavey Ark	697m/2287ft	Langdale
Pike o'Blisco	705m/2313ft	Langdale
Pike o'Stickle	708m/2323ft	Langdale
Pillar	892m/2926ft	Wasdale
Place Fell	657m/2155ft	Mardale and the Far East
Raise	884m/2900ft	Patterdale
Rampsgill Head	792m/2598ft	Mardale and the Far East
Rannerdale Knotts	355m/1165ft	Buttermere
Raven Crag	463m/1519ft	Borrowdale
Red Pike (Buttermere)	755m/2477ft	Buttermere
Red Pike (Wasdale)	828m/2717ft	Wasdale
Red Screes	777m/2549ft	Patterdale
Rest Dodd	697m/2287ft	Mardale and the Far East
Robinson	737m/2418ft	Buttermere
Rossett Pike	651m/2136ft	Langdale

Fell name	Height	Volume
Rosthwaite Fell	551m/1808ft	Borrowdale
Sail	771m/2529ft	Buttermere
Sale Fell	359m/1178ft	Keswick
Sallows	516m/1693ft	Mardale and the Far East
Scafell	964m/3163ft	Wasdale
Scafell Pike	977m/3206ft	Borrowdale, Langdale, Wasdale
Scar Crags	672m/2205ft	Buttermere
Scoat Fell	843m/2766ft	Wasdale
Seatallan	693m/2274ft	Wasdale
Seathwaite Fell	631m/2070ft	Borrowdale
Seat Sandal	736m/2415ft	Patterdale
Selside Pike	655m/2149ft	Mardale and the Far East
Sergeant Man	736m/2414ft	Langdale
Sergeant's Crag	574m/1883ft	Borrowdale
Sheffield Pike	675m/2215ft	Patterdale
Shipman Knotts	587m/1926ft	Mardale and the Far East
Silver How	395m/1296ft	Langdale
Skiddaw	931m/3054ft	Keswick
Skiddaw Little Man	865m/2838ft	Keswick
Slight Side	762m/2500ft	Wasdale
Souther Fell	522m/1713ft	Keswick
Stainton Pike	498m/1634ft	Coniston
Starling Dodd	635m/2083ft	Buttermere
Steel Fell	553m/1814ft	Langdale
Steel Knotts	433m/1421ft	Mardale and the Far East
Steeple	819m/2687ft	Wasdale
Stickle Pike	376m/1234ft	Coniston
Stone Arthur	503m/1650ft	Patterdale

Fell name	Height	Volume
St Sunday Crag	841m/2759ft	Patterdale
Stybarrow Dodd	846m/2776ft	Patterdale
Swirl How	804m/2638ft	Coniston
Tarn Crag (Easedale)	485m/1591ft	Langdale
Tarn Crag (Longsleddale)	664m/2179ft	Mardale and the Far East
Thornthwaite Crag	784m/2572ft	Mardale and the Far East
Thunacar Knott	723m/2372ft	Langdale
Troutbeck Tongue	363m/1191ft	Mardale and the Far East
Ullock Pike	690m/2264ft	Keswick
Ullscarf	726m/2382ft	Borrowdale
Walla Crag	379m/1243ft	Borrowdale
Wallowbarrow Crag	292m/958ft	Coniston
Walna Scar	621m/2037ft	Coniston
Wandope	772m/2533ft	Buttermere
Wansfell	489m/1604ft	Mardale and the Far East
Watson's Dodd	789m/2589ft	Patterdale
Wether Hill	673m/2208ft	Mardale and the Far East
Wetherlam	762m/2500ft	Coniston
Whinfell Beacon	472m/1549ft	Mardale and the Far East
Whinlatter	517m/1696ft	Keswick
Whin Rigg	536m/1759ft	Wasdale
Whiteless Pike	660m/2165ft	Buttermere
Whiteside	707m/2320ft	Buttermere
White Side	863m/2831ft	Patterdale
Whitfell	573m/1880ft	Coniston
Winterscleugh	464m/1522ft	Mardale and the Far East
Yewbarrow	628m/2060ft	Wasdale
Yoadcastle	494m/1621ft	Coniston
Yoke	706m/2316ft	Mardale and the Far East

LISTING OF CICERONE GUIDES

LISTING OF CICERONE GUIDES *continued*

DERBYSHIRE, PEAK DISTRICT AND MIDLANDS

Cycling in the Peak District
Dark Peak Walks
Scrambles in the Dark Peak
Walking in Derbyshire
Walking in the Peak District – White Peak East
White Peak Walks: The Southern Dales

SOUTHERN ENGLAND

20 Classic Sportive Rides in South East England
20 Classic Sportive Rides in South West England
Cycling in the Cotswolds
Mountain Biking on the North Downs
Mountain Biking on the South Downs
Suffolk Coast and Heath Walks
The Cotswold Way
The Cotswold Way Map Booklet
The Great Stones Way
The Kennet and Avon Canal
The Lea Valley Walk
The North Downs Way
The North Downs Way Map Booklet
The Peddars Way and Norfolk Coast Path
The Pilgrims' Way
The Ridgeway National Trail
The Ridgeway Map Booklet
The South Downs Way
The South Downs Way Map Booklet
The South West Coast Path
The South West Coast Path Map Booklet – Vol 1: Minehead to St Ives
The South West Coast Path Map Booklet – Vol 2: St Ives to Plymouth
The South West Coast Path Map Booklet – Vol 3: Plymouth to Poole
The Thames Path
The Thames Path Map Booklet
The Two Moors Way
The Two Moors Way Map Booklet
Walking Hampshire's Test Way
Walking in Cornwall
Walking in Essex
Walking in Kent
Walking in London
Walking in Norfolk
Walking in the Chilterns
Walking in the Cotswolds
Walking in the Isles of Scilly
Walking in the New Forest
Walking in the North Wessex Downs
Walking in the Thames Valley
Walking on Dartmoor
Walking on Guernsey
Walking on Jersey
Walking on the Isle of Wight

Walking the Jurassic Coast
Walks in the South Downs National Park

BRITISH ISLES CHALLENGES, COLLECTIONS AND ACTIVITIES

The Big Rounds
The Book of the Bivvy
The Book of the Bothy
The C2C Cycle Route
The End to End Cycle Route
The Mountains of England and Wales: Vol 1 Wales
The Mountains of England and Wales: Vol 2 England
The National Trails
Three Peaks, Ten Tors
Walking The End to End Trail

ALPS CROSS-BORDER ROUTES

100 Hut Walks in the Alps
Alpine Ski Mountaineering Vol 1 – Western Alps
Alpine Ski Mountaineering Vol 2 – Central and Eastern Alps
Chamonix to Zermatt
The Karnischer Hohenweg
The Tour of the Bernina
Tour of Monte Rosa
Tour of the Matterhorn
Trail Running – Chamonix and the Mont Blanc region
Trekking in the Alps
Trekking in the Silvretta and Ratikon Alps
Trekking Munich to Venice
Trekking the Tour of Mont Blanc
Walking in the Alps

PYRENEES AND FRANCE/SPAIN CROSS-BORDER ROUTES

Shorter Treks in the Pyrenees
The GR10 Trail
The GR11 Trail
The Pyrenean Haute Route
The Pyrenees
Walks and Climbs in the Pyrenees

AUSTRIA

Innsbruck Mountain Adventures
The Adlerweg
Trekking in Austria's Hohe Tauern
Trekking in the Stubai Alps
Trekking in the Zillertal Alps
Walking in Austria

SWITZERLAND

Switzerland's Jura Crest Trail
The Swiss Alpine Pass Route – Via Alpina Route 1
The Swiss Alps
Tour of the Jungfrau Region
Walking in the Bernese Oberland

Walking in the Engadine – Switzerland
Walking in the Valais

FRANCE

Chamonix Mountain Adventures
Cycle Touring in France
Cycling London to Paris
Cycling the Canal de la Garonne
Cycling the Canal du Midi
Mont Blanc Walks
Mountain Adventures in the Maurienne
The GR20 Corsica
The GR5 Trail
The GR5 Trail – Vosges and Jura
The Grand Traverse of the Massif Central
The Loire Cycle Route
The Moselle Cycle Route
The River Rhone Cycle Route
The Robert Louis Stevenson Trail
The Way of St James – Le Puy to the Pyrenees
Tour of the Oisans: The GR54
Tour of the Queyras
Vanoise Ski Touring
Via Ferratas of the French Alps
Walking in Corsica
Walking in Provence – East
Walking in Provence – West
Walking in the Auvergne
Walking in the Brianconnais
Walking in the Dordogne
Walking in the Haute Savoie: North
Walking in the Haute Savoie: South

GERMANY

Hiking and Cycling in the Black Forest
The Danube Cycleway Vol 1
The Rhine Cycle Route
The Westweg
Walking in the Bavarian Alps

ICELAND AND GREENLAND

Trekking in Greenland – The Arctic Circle Trail
Walking and Trekking in Iceland

IRELAND

The Wild Atlantic Way and Western Ireland

ITALY

Italy's Sibillini National Park
Shorter Walks in the Dolomites
Ski Touring and Snowshoeing in the Dolomites
The Way of St Francis
Trekking in the Apennines
Trekking in the Dolomites
Via Ferratas of the Italian Dolomites Vols 1 & 2
Walking and Trekking in the Gran Paradiso

For full information on all our guides,
books and eBooks, visit our website:
www.cicerone.co.uk

Explore the world with Cicerone

**walking • trekking • mountaineering • climbing • mountain biking •
cycling • via ferratas • scrambling • trail running • skills and techniques**

For over 50 years, Cicerone have built up an outstanding collection of
nearly 400 guides, inspiring all sorts of amazing experiences.

www.cicerone.co.uk – where adventures begin

- Our **website** is a treasure-trove for every outdoor adventurer. You
  can buy books or read inspiring articles and trip reports, get technical
  advice, check for updates, and view videos, photographs and mapping
  for routes and treks.

- **Register this book** or any other Cicerone guide in your member's
  library on our website and you can choose to automatically access
  updates and GPX files for your books, if available.

- Our **fortnightly newsletters** will update you on new publications and
  articles and keep you informed of other news and events. You can also
  follow us on Facebook, Twitter and Instagram.

We hope you have enjoyed using this guidebook. If you have any
comments you would like to share, please contact us using the form on
our website or via email, so that we can provide the best experience for
future customers.

CICERONE

Juniper House, Murley Moss Business Village, Oxenholme Road, Kendal LA9 7RL

✉ info@cicerone.co.uk   cicerone.co.uk